Why Can't You Be

D0689413

Why Can't You Behave?

The Teacher's Guide to
Creative Classroom Management, K–3

Paula Rogovin

HEINEMANN
Portsmouth, NH

Heinemann
A division of Reed Elsevier Inc.
361 Hanover Street
Portsmouth, NH 03801–3912
www.heinemann.com

Offices and agents throughout the world

© 2004 by Paula Rogovin

All rights reserved. No part of this book may be reproduced in any form or by any electronic or mechanical means, including information storage and retrieval systems, without permission in writing from the publisher, except by a reviewer, who may quote brief passages in a review.

Library of Congress Cataloging-in-Publication Data
Rogovin, Paula.
    Why can't you behave? : the teacher's guide to creative
classroom management, K–3 / Paula Rogovin.
        p.   cm.
    Includes bibliographical references and index.
    ISBN 0-325-00651-2 (alk. paper)
    1. Classroom management.   2. School discipline.   3. Education, Primary.   I. Title.

LB3013.R59 2004
371.102'4—dc22   2004004322

Editor: Lois Bridges
Production coordinator: Elizabeth Valway
Production service: Denise Botelho
Cover design: Night & Day Design
Composition: Publishers' Design and Production Services, Inc.
Manufacturing: Steve Bernier

Printed in the United States of America on acid-free paper
08 07 06 05 04   EB   1 2 3 4 5

This book is dedicated to my mother, Anne Rogovin, who died from brain cancer on July 7, 2003, after a brief and painless illness.

Mom, you have always been and will always be in my heart, in my teaching, in my life. I love you and miss you.

Contents

Acknowledgments

After all the graduate courses taken and the books read, perhaps my greatest learning came from my students. It wasn't really the "easy" ones, the ones who loved to learn, to participate, to share, and to follow the rules, who were my greatest teachers (though I loved them all the same). Rather, it was those children who were more complicated, the ones who made me lose sleep at night, the ones who forced me to turn to families and colleagues for help. They were the ones I pondered about with my dear friend and colleague, Isabel Beaton, over dinner at Bistango Restaurant on many a Friday evening. I must thank my students.

Children can certainly tell us when we've done a great lesson, or when our curriculum doesn't meet their needs or learning styles. The expression, or lack thereof, on their faces can tell us if they're with us or lost in thought. Their expressions of joy, their intense involvement in learning and community, inform and energize us. They can teach us a whole lot—if we're looking and listening. We can learn to do better if we're willing to be learners and researchers as we teach.

Thank you to the families of my students. You helped me learn the importance of placing family life and culture in the center of my teaching. Your participation within and outside of the classroom has enriched my teaching and my life. The list of those family members with whom I feel so close would fill many pages. Just know that I truly love and appreciate you.

Thank you to my colleagues from the three New York City Public Schools where I have worked over the last thirty-one years—from P.S. 132 and P.S. 173, in Washington Heights, and The Manhattan New School (P.S. 290) (MNS) on the East Side. Thanks to my colleagues and friends, the teachers, custodians, paraprofessionals, guidance counselors, lunchroom staff, adminstrative staff, student teachers, teaching assistants, and administrators.

Dora Cruz (school aide), Dolores Buonasora (teaching assistant), and Petrana Koutcheva (paraprofessional) are three extraordinary human beings who have worked in our classroom at The Manhattan New School. We shared our love of teaching, our families, our lives. Thank you.

Thanks to Isabel Beaton, Carmen Colon, Jordan Forstat, Regina Chiou, Lisa Seigman, and Pam Mayer. How many endless hours did we hang out in our class-rooms, homes, and restaurants from early morning till late at night, talking about our students, sharing our stories, agonizing over the problems, and beaming over progress?

Lois Bridges, my editor and friend at Heinemann, is a spectacular human being. It was a suggestion from Lois that really got me thinking about the need for this book about discipline and classroom management. My first two Heinemann books focused on curriculum issues. How can you develop a rich curriculum with-out classroom management skills? How can you possibly work on discipline in a classroom where there's nothing "cooking" in the curriculum, where children are not deeply involved in learning? Yes, curriculum and classroom management skills are both essential. Thank you Lois, for encouraging me to write this book and for helping me through the process. Thanks for your many emails about the trials and tribulations of the public school system and your concerns for peace and justice in the world. There's a strong bond of caring that reaches from here in New York City all the way to your home in California. Thank you for your friendship and support.

Thanks to the many people at the Teachers College Writing Project who opened me to the concept of being a teacher-researcher, who enabled me to see teaching as a process, not an end.

Thanks to Shelley Harwayne, whom I met through the Writing Project. Shel-ley has been my mentor, my principal at The Manhattan New School, my Super-intendent in District 2, my friend, and my inspiration. Shelley changed my life. It was Shelley who taught me to reflect deeply on my teaching, who taught me so much about education and humanity, and who insisted that I teach at MNS. It was Shelley's invitation to work at MNS that provided an opportunity for me to teach to my heart's content, without the "shackles" of a proscribed curriculum. It was Shelley who urged me to document and share my teaching in books and videos. I wish her happiness and good health in her retirement.

Thanks to my own family, my sons, David, Steven, and Eric, whom I love with all my heart and soul. Love and thanks to my sister, Ellen, and her daughters, Aliya and Malaika, and her children, Hoshea and Yacob, to my brother Mark and his wife, Michelle, for all of their love and support. We were together with Milton and Anne, during the illness and death of Anne—singing, reading poetry, dancing, writing, talking, laughing, demonstrating for peace, holding hands, and crying.

Dad, you are rock solid. You brought values, politics, art, poetry, music, love and joy into my life. I will always seek to share that with my students. I love you.

To my friends, I deeply value your friendship and support: Mary Trefethan Segall (friend for forty-two years) and Seth Segall; Lisa Brand; Linda, and her late father, Lloyd Brown; Ilene and Jim Gilbert; Marie, Steve, and Matthew Chaseman; Maria, Caesar, Raquel, Jason, and Michelle Munive; Janice, Ed, and Jenna Dabney; Laurie Finkelstein; Hallie Wannamaker and Vincent Brevetti; Ann Sadowski and Joe Cassidy; Carol Hutchens; Micheal Milano; Marie, John, and Joe Fuchida; Naomi, Tom, and Ben Blumenfeld; Bea, Steve, Rebecca, and David Gopoian; David Heatley; Sara, Bob, Denise, Arthur, and Errol Rubenstein; Michael Milano; Maria Castillo; Nancy, Marty, and Gary Willick; Gail and Sarah Gordon; Bertha Small; Minetha Spence; Keila and Neil Schulman; Joan Stein; and Ann Zalesky.

Thanks to my friend Mark Greenberg for the long walks and talks and hours of music-making and for your love and support.

Thanks to my dear friend and colleague Isabel Beaton, a real treasure to humanity. I wish you well in your retirement.

Thanks to Anthony Avellino, parent of former students Julie and Lia, and manager of Bistango Restaurant, for setting aside that candlelit corner of your restaurant where my colleagues, family, and friends gathered on many a night. The food and your hospitality certainly helped improve the quality and intensity of all of our teaching and our lives.

Thanks to Esther Nuñez, Molly Bass, and to our many other student teachers. I wish you joy in your teaching.

To all the people my class interviewed over the years—family members, workers, neighbors, colleagues, poets and writers, artists, and scientists Nora Guthrie, Rachel Robinson, Vera B. Williams, Bobby DeCola, Carlton Green, Brian Pinkney—you have been such fine role models for us. Thank you. You have taught and inspired us.

1

Discipline—Making It Happen in Your Classroom

I admit I cried nearly every day during my first year of teaching. I just couldn't accomplish what I wanted because the children just wouldn't behave the way I wanted. There was calling out, fooling around, and more. Does that sound familiar? In my first five years of teaching, I happened to be at a school where screaming was the main way to enforce the rules. My positive experiences during student teaching were just not enough, given classes of thirty-five first graders and no support. I hated to scream, but saw few other options.

Quite soon, I realized that screaming just wouldn't work. Screaming is an assault to the ears and an assault on one's being. Screaming, directed at one child, ends up rattling the nerves of the whole class. Screaming is intimidating to all—not just to the intended victim. Also, screaming stops the flow of work in the classroom. Screaming just isn't effective. And, what can you do after you scream? There is nowhere to go.

There must be other ways. I yearned to teach without the constant strain from dealing with classroom management. I made it my responsibility to develop new strategies and new techniques. I was determined to turn my teaching around. What did I learn? I will share my thinking and practice in hopes that it will be helpful to you.

In this chapter I will answer these questions:

- What are discipline and classroom management?
- How are discipline and curriculum related?
- How can we make classroom management effective?
- Is the classroom a democracy?
- How can we empower children?
- How can we establish discipline in the classroom?
- How can we enforce the rules?

What Are Discipline and Classroom Management?

Classroom management is the creation of a system for working towards or approximating a certain kind of conduct or action, a certain kind of discipline. Discipline involves learned behavior, both for the teacher and the students. Classroom management involves dealing with previously learned behavior and familial and societal influences. It involves dealing with teacher's and children's physical health and emotional well-being. It involves dealing with the concrete realities of a school—the class size, the room size, the particular combination of students, the availability of supplies and resources, and the availability of support.

Classroom management requires strategic problem solving aimed at bringing about particular types of behaviors. These behaviors are needed so that there can be effective teaching and learning. It involves teachers and students being researchers as they seek to establish guidelines and solve problems. As researchers, teachers and children need to ask:

What is the problem at hand?

How can I, or how can we, solve the problem?

What structures, routines and rituals, and supports will enable that problem solving?

What are the limitations in this situation?

What responsibilities do I want to turn over to my students, while still helping them feel safe and secure?

What strategies and techniques can we use to implement our goals?

Sometimes the solution requires the involvement of people outside of the classroom—families, guidance counselors, or administrators. How should we involve these people?

In my first few years of teaching, I didn't think strategically, and I had few management techniques to draw on. How did I change my ways? I thought. I read. I looked for mentors both within my school and among teacher-friends. I watched other teachers very closely. I talked with my sister, Ellen Rogovin Hart, a teacher in Philadelphia. Over the years I tried different strategies and techniques I had learned from others. I used those techniques that worked for me.

Here is an example. I had stopped shouting after my first few years. I never cared for saying, "Sh, sh," ringing bells, or turning lights off to get the children's attention. When I arrived at The Manhattan New School in 1994, I observed a teacher who got her class to stop working or talking by doing a rhythmical clap—da_____, da_____, da, da, da. Her class responded with the same clap. Then there was silence. I just loved that. I tried it, and it worked for me. But, one day, a parent from another class at The Manhattan New School was showing my students some African dance steps. She said to my students in Swahili, *"Ago"* (pronounced AH-go). She said it in a quiet, song-like way, and then told the children what it meant, "I want your attention." She taught them the response, *"Ame"* (AH-may), "We are listening." She had the children practice it once, and then she proceeded with the lesson. After that moment, I never went back to the clapping. This was it for me. It helped me set the respectful tone I wanted for my class, as these Swahili terms were melodic and calming. The low volume of these words seems to cut through or below the typical classroom talk or chatter. When children are working quietly, *"Ago"* gets them to stop and look at the teacher without startling or jarring them. Shelley Harwayne talks about "Humanely Bringing a Class to Attention" in her book *Going Public, Priorities and Practice at The Manhattan New School.* She says, "You can't have a healthy school culture without the careful use of language" (1999, 122–23). I would extend this to the whole area of classroom management.

How Are Discipline and Curriculum Related?

Discipline and curriculum are intertwined. To develop a curriculum, there must be guidelines for behavior and for interaction among the students and interaction between students and the adults. But, discipline without a rich curriculum spells disaster! A limited curriculum, a dull curriculum, an uninspired curriculum is boring (a word I don't like at all). How can we possibly expect children to "behave nicely" with such a curriculum? It's not fair. It's torturous.

I have seen proof of this over the years when I have observed children in classes with limited or cookie-cutter or templated-one-size-fits-all curriculums handed to teachers by school districts. Some of the children just adapt to the classroom; others respond by misbehaving. When these same children enter a class that has a rich curriculum, the behavior problems usually phase out. I have seen some of the most disruptive and difficult children become entranced with inquiry studies. I had a child in my first grade class who bit, kicked, spit, and disrupted his kindergarten class. He had a new teacher who had a very limited curriculum. The child just didn't know what to do with himself, so he acted out and disrupted. In contrast, he was in love with the research in our first grade class and was a brilliant and active participant. We saw absolutely no negative behavior from him in class. In fact, he wrote a poem called "My Face Is One Big Smile." He truly needed full curriculum. I have had teachers deliberately send difficult children to my class because "your curriculum will be good for him."

How Can We Make Classroom Management Effective?

Classroom management requires a positive attitude, and the teacher sets the tone. I love teaching. I love children. That's important. My students and their families feel that love. (If a teacher is in this field just for the shorter hours, the summer vacations, or the salary, it's not the right field. It's not good for the children. And, they can feel it.) No matter which children or family members end up in my class, I believe that I must seek to be the best teacher for the children. I must seek to find ways to reach and teach every child to the best of my ability.

The teacher comes to the classroom with a set of values that indicate what style of working and learning there will be (once she develops classroom management techniques that work for her). I want to learn from the children and their families. I want to empower children to learn from people and the environment around them. I want both children and teachers to be caring and supportive of people within and outside of the school. Since I want the classroom to be a community of learners, a community of people working cooperatively, we have to treat each other in a way that helps build that community. Both the children and the teacher have to be respectful of each other.

In the 1980s, I met many teachers and staff developers through the Writing Project at Teachers College and watched them interact with children. I was overjoyed to hear the calm, gentle tone of Georgia Heard, as she worked with my class and with other teachers. Georgia, a marvelous poet, was working at that time as a staff developer for the Writing Project. I noticed that we could hear her quiet tone right through the louder chatter of the children. I noticed the calming effect of her voice, and the voices of Joanne Portalupi and other Writing Project staff developers. My students responded so well to their low-volume, calm voices and listened well to what was said. The staff developers inspired my students to write. It was almost as if the children felt those low voices and the ideas they brought were respectful of them. I believe that an important part of discipline is teachers showing respect for their students.

Is the Classroom a Democracy?

The classroom should be democratic, but it is not a democracy. This may sound like a contradiction in terms, but it is not. I am the teacher. I am in charge of the class. Many of the basic rules are rules from the Board of Education or guidelines from our school administration. The rest of the basic rules are my rules. The children work within the basic rules. They can participate in developing additional rules, guidelines, or practices for our class.

In the United States, our Constitution sets the basic rules for our democracy. The Congress and the state and city governing boards establish other laws and rules. In still other matters, individuals are free to do as they wish, as long as the laws are upheld. The children are like members of those governing boards and individual citizens.

Just as in the U.S. form of democracy, I am not offering total freedom of choice. When a child wants to be in charge or dominate our class, it is unacceptable. When a child finishes another child's sentences or my sentences, as if they are better than us, it is unacceptable. If a bunch of children want to be mean and exclusive, it is unacceptable. If some children don't like disabled children or children of other races, nationalities, or economic groups, any behavior that shows that dislike is unacceptable. This reflects my basic rules. These rules include:

- Meanness, arrogance (making others think you are better than they or that they are not important or intelligent), and prejudice are unacceptable.
- Students and adults must be respectful of each other as people and as learners.
- Solving problems through violence is unacceptable.
- Seeking multiple strategies for problem solving is important.
- Each person must participate in maintaining the classroom.
- Everyone must do their academic work to the best of their ability.
- Everyone has the right to participate and should be encouraged to do so.
- We must try our best to help each other.

As teacher, I want to set the tone just as a parent sets the tone and values for a family. As teacher, I want to develop the values of caring, support, fairness, justice, democracy, and the right of all children in the class to a quality education. Also, I want the children to feel safe and secure knowing that there is a responsible adult in charge.

Children must be made aware that rules (whether the rules were set by the adults or arrived at by the class) must be followed. One of the worst things I see parents or teachers doing is letting their children negotiate everything. You'll hear, "But Mommy. . . ." Or you'll see tantrums, whining, or fussing. Allowing these behaviors is counterproductive. There are certain basic rules that must be followed. Sometimes you will hear me say, "Our rule about talking in the stairway did not change." Or, "Our rule about interrupting other children is still the same. You may not do that." Or, "You can't just sit and talk. You must do your writing at Writing Workshop. If you don't do it now, you will have to do it at Center Time." I make it very clear that tantrums, whining, and fussing are totally unacceptable and will not make me change our rules or my expectations. What about the democratic part of this? I want all children in the class to be able to:

- participate fully in discussions and activities
- be free of harassment or intimidation
- express opinions, even if they differ with mine or those of other children
- get as much support as possible for their learning
- get a quality education whether or not their family supports that effort
- get a quality education whether or not the teacher(s) like the child
- make the greatest progress possible—realizing that children come to the classroom with different life experiences, skills, and abilities
- feel empowered to take charge of their learning and behavior within the guidelines established by the teacher and the class
- help establish *some* of the rules or guidelines. Children can even discuss problems, objections, and concerns with rules and make suggestions for changes to existing rules.
- seek answers to their questions
- be treated fairly. Sometimes children are justifiably concerned about the unfair enforcement of the rules. For example, a girl may have a lighter punishment than a boy; the son of the PTA president may not be treated the same as other children; a child who is frequently in trouble may have a harsher consequence than another child; or the teacher may not look into a child's grievance in great enough depth to find out what really happened. We must make every effort to avoid that sexism or favoritism and be fair.

The issue of negotiable issues is quite interesting. In a democracy, social activists deliberately break laws in order to point out the problems in the laws and to push for new laws. As an activist I sat-in and even got arrested to force the City of New York to provide funding for child care centers in the 1970s. We broke the no-trespassing law but had our sentences suspended, and we won the funding. As an activist I was arrested with other teachers who blocked the entrance to the South African Consulate in an effort to end apartheid.

How can children work to change the rules? My students know they may not throw tantrums, whine, or cry to bring about changes in our classroom rules. I certainly don't encourage sit-ins or other such actions in our classroom. I don't even encourage discussions about changing the *basic* rules because we have so many curriculum issues to attend to. I have the right to say, "We are not changing that rule." For example, I wouldn't want to change our rule about being mean to other children. After an explanation, I will tell the class that this rule is nonnegotiable. However, if the children are still concerned about a rule, they should be able to discuss this with me or with the whole class.

Children in my class do have the right to question a rule or a practice. Sometimes I have looked at a rule and have realized that a particular rule or practice is not appropriate or useful and will change it.

Individual children or a group of children can modify a rule or practice by talking to me or writing a note to me. They can also talk with their family who may then approach me about a rule or a practice. I will then talk with one child, family members, a group of children, or we will have a class discussion about a rule that seems problematic. Just as families have to find ways to negotiate, so do students and teachers.

Problem solving is our forte. Frequently I pose questions so that children can construct solutions. Various children propose solutions. We listen to each other and then put the best of those ideas together to formulate a solution, for example, if I ask, "How can we help _____ (a child who is new in our class) feel welcome?" One child might say, "I'll play with him at recess." Another might say, "I'll show him where to get his school lunch." Someone might say, "He can have lunch with _____ and me." Someone else might offer to show the child where to hang up his coat. If someone says, "We should be nice to him," I might ask, "What does that mean, what can we do to be nice to someone?" (so that it's not just empty words). With these suggestions, we have constructed a solution to that problem. I praise the children for their thoughtfulness. I will ask after lunch what actually happened in the lunch room and yard. I praise the children who actually took the time to be helpful and supportive to the new child.

Sometimes we will have a class discussion to help formulate a new rule or procedure for solving a problem. For example, our coatroom is tiny. Some children fool around there, and it can become overcrowded, uncomfortable, and even dangerous. We already had a no-fooling-around rule. We talked about the problems, and constructed some new rules for use of the closet: We established one side for going in and one for going out. Children made arrows which we taped on the floor. Only five children can go in at one time. You have to take your coat off before you enter. You put your coat back on outside of the closet. That's so you can go in and out quickly.

How Can We Empower Children?

We need to believe in the empowerment of children. Then we need to make a commitment to find ways we can make that happen. Many teachers get caught up with being the sole power in the classroom. They are in charge, they are the holders of the information, they control the piece of the curriculum the administration allows them to control. The thought of ceding some power (over curriculum or discipline) to young children is unimaginable.

Children should feel empowered. One responsibility I have as the teacher is to shift *some* of the power to the children—to empower them. I want children to take over as much of the governance of their own behavior as possible, while I enable them to feel safe and secure.

Empowering Children to Be in Charge of Their Own Behavior

My goal is to have the children be the enforcers of their own behavior. I often say, "You are in charge of your own behavior." I want the children not only to help formulate some of the rules or procedures and to internalize the rules, but to be responsible for monitoring themselves. The children will often hear me say these words:

> You are the teacher.
> You are in charge of your behavior. That's not my job.
> It's your responsibility to remember to bring your pencil. (If I have told the children to go to Reading Workshop with a journal and a pencil, I don't want to remind anyone to bring a pencil.)
> You must remind yourself to be silent when someone else is talking. That's your responsibility.
> I don't want to remind you not to call out. You are in charge of your behavior.
> Be your own teacher.

This works. Most children will take that responsibility over time. Sometimes they must be reminded ahead of time and complimented (not thanked) often, but not every time. "You kids are terrific. You were so quiet and respectful of the other classes when you were walking in the hallway." If another teacher mentions that my children were so helpful to each other, I make a big deal out of that. "I'm so proud of you, boys and girls. You are so great." Most children will respond well to this approach. You will see a gradual and positive change.

Of course, there are the children who will need constant reminders—the quiet reminders, the stern, low-volume reminders, and so on. They may need those reminders for half of the year. I had one child (we'll call him Brian) who called out every single answer. He was bright and usually had appropriate answers, but we have a rule that kids can't call out answers during discussions. I spoke to him about his responsibility to give other children a chance to answer questions. I spoke to him quietly. I even spoke to him once in front of the whole class so that the other children would see that I was taking steps to correct Brian's behavior. His mother thought there was nothing wrong with this behavior. In fact, she encouraged him to be bold at home where there were two older siblings. I figured out a way to approach the problem. When other children raised their hands and stopped calling out, I praised them in front of the class. "Anna used to call out all of the time. I am so pleased that she is raising her hand now. That's great. Now other children are getting a chance to answer questions. Let's give Anna a hand." Kids love to be praised. Before long, Brian stopped calling out. When I complimented him, the whole class applauded.

The combination of these strategies usually brings about positive results regarding behavior:

- reminders to the class before an activity
- quiet talks with individual children
- a talk with family
- compliments to children for their improved behavior, quietly and/or in front of the class
- a consequence for inappropriate behavior
- sending a child who has improved to a colleague or to the principal for additional praise

Often I joke with the children and say,

You took my job away. I thought I was supposed to tell you to bring your journal to Research Workshop.

You took my job away. I thought I was supposed to tell you to help with the cleanup (or to move you away from someone you think you will talk with instead of doing your work).

Sometimes I even say,

Well, I guess I can go on vacation now, you don't need me to be in charge of Writing Workshop (or other activity).

Whenever I say these words, the children laugh because they know I am so happy when they take my jobs away. They love the feeling of being in charge, of being empowered.

Empowering Children to Be in Charge of Their Learning

Yes, I want to empower the children to be in charge of their behavior and their learning. I want them to learn and to *teach* as much as possible. That's why at Research, Reading, Math, and Writing Workshops we work, not on reciting the right answer but, we work on strategies. At Research Workshop we look at our prior knowledge, ask questions, and find many ways to search for answers. We work cooperatively to construct answers.

At Reading Workshop, rather than telling children the word they don't know, we work on strategies for figuring out new words (look at the picture, sound out the word, skip the word and come back to it, look at patterns, etc.). Then they can use those strategies without depending on an adult or a classmate.

We work on strategies for spelling such as sounding out words, looking for words on our word walls, looking for words on the labels for our murals, finding words on signs and posters in the room, or remembering where we saw the word before. This puts the children in charge when they are writing pages for their homemade books about interviews or when they are at Writing Workshop. I don't want children pulling on my shirt asking me how to spell words. Often, I look up from conferencing with a child, and I look around the room. It's a beautiful sight. Some children are standing at the word wall copying the spelling of a particular word. Some children are looking in their journal or in a book where they know they can find a word. Some children are deeply involved in writing a poem or a story. They may stop by the poetry books to look at a poem that is important to them. Some have walked over to the writing center to get more paper or to staple pages together. A few children are working on stories together, so you can hear the hum of their voices. It's calm and peaceful and rigorous. They are in charge of their behavior and their writing.

At Math Workshop, I ask children to come over to the board or the screen for the overhead projector to be the teacher. Often, I will say that we want to know how they chose to solve a problem. I expect them to explain their math thinking step by step. I compliment them for their math thinking and their teaching skills. I compliment other children for their good listening.

There are times when it feels like a college classroom. That's when the children have taken over responsibility for their own work and their behavior. That's when the rituals and routines have been internalized. That's when children feel confident that their needs are being met by the teacher and the class—the classroom community. Many a time I have said to them, "Wow, I was watching you write today. It feels just like a college class." I name those college-like behaviors and compliment the children. Oh, do they feel great when I say that!

How Can We Establish Discipline in the Classroom?

Setting the Guidelines for Acceptable Behavior

Setting guidelines and standards begins the first moment we meet our new class. We do not use the first month just to teach the rules, as is done in many classrooms. Rather, the rules evolve as we engage in our work. In our class, we dig into our curriculum immediately. The following is an example of how we do this at the beginning of the school year. As you follow us through time, in this and subsequent chapters, you will see how our rules and guidelines *evolve*.

LEARNING NAMES

At Manhattan New School, we meet our class in the school yard. I'm out early the first day of school to greet the children and their families or babysitters. We (student teachers, paraprofessionals, teaching assistants, family members, or whoever will be working in our classroom that year) give children their name tags. That helps us learn their names, a task I want to accomplish by the end of the first day. (I have written their names on cubbies, mailboxes, and on various lists in my computer. So I just need to match the children with their names.) It also helps the children learn each other's names. I think it's a sign of respect to call someone by their name.

At MNS, we use first names, for children and adults. When children don't know each other's names early in the school year, they can point to them with a hand, not a finger, or say, "him" or "her," and I quickly remind them of the child's name. Learning names isn't always easy, so we need to find ways to support that learning.

Whether we use first or last names is not important. Respect is earned. Using the correct name is important to me. Many teachers change difficult or foreign-sounding names or abbreviate long names. I repeat names that are difficult to me over and over to myself or write them out phonetically until I get them right. I try to find out what name the family uses and what the child and/or family wants me to use.

When an unusual name comes up in the course of our day, whether it is a real person or someone in a story, *laughing at the name is unacceptable*. We talk about this when it first happens and then whenever necessary.

USING PLEASANT, WELCOMING SIGNALS

Then comes the train whistle, which, for me, is far more pleasant than bull horns, whistles, or adults screaming at children to get in line. The train whistle for me is a symbol of a journey—of our days together that will certainly be a journey. It also means stop playing in the yard and come to line up. I'll use this whistle every morning. I help each child find a partner. It's not a great line, and I don't expect it to be, because we haven't established official partners for the month or any getting-in-line guidelines. I encourage the families to join us in the classroom that first day of school.

USING CALM, LOW VOICES

When we get in line, and when we come into the classroom, my voice is quiet and calm. From the first minute, I am setting an example for one of our important guidelines. We keep the volume of our voices low and without sharp edges. Most of the children will respond with low-volume voices. I will continue to be a role model for this throughout the year. Occasionally I will have to remind a child or the whole class about the low-volume voices. Occasionally there will be a child who needs work to take the sharp edge out of her voice.

MAKING DIRECTIONS CLEAR

Before we come into the room that first day, we stop. I tell the children to look at me and listen. I focus my eyes on the children and speak in a calm, low voice. I greet the children. Then I tell them what I expect them to do with their jackets, book bags, or other school supplies. (The first day I have already placed chairs at the tables because I haven't yet shown them how I expect them to carry the chairs safely from the stacks to the tables, one at a time. I will show them how to carry chairs safely when we clean up at the end of the first day.) I tell them to go to sit on the carpet at story circle. I ask family members to help us put the children's names and room number on book bags and lunch boxes. *This stopping to present directions or expectations is a routine that we will do every day, in the morning and before each transition.* Children need to know what you expect them to do.

MAKING CHILDREN FEEL WELCOME

As children enter the room, I try to quietly acknowledge the presence of each child with a quick hello, a question, a wave, or a smile. We will always have time for that as they hang up coats, put folders in the mailboxes, and put the chairs at tables in subsequent days.

MAKING FAMILIES FEEL WELCOME AND COMFORTABLE

The children come over to the carpet at story circle. Family members sit and stand all over the room, while I sit on the rocking chair to welcome everyone. I want to use this opportunity to set the tone for the year. I say quietly, *"Ago."* Children who have heard the words from the Swahili language while in kindergarten know the response—*"Ame."* For those who don't know, I explain. It's now quiet.

I tell the families that they are my coworkers and that they are welcome in our room. Family members introduce themselves. I tell them a little about our upcoming block study (or whatever our major social studies theme will be). Already on the first day, the families see that we will be getting right to work with our studies. Then, I take out my guitar, and we sing Woody Guthrie's song, "This Land Is Your Land," and a few other songs. I see smiles and a sense of relief on the faces of family members who don't already know me. The bulletin boards are backed with colorful paper, just awaiting the children's work. The room is clean and orderly, with pencils, crayons, and markers on each work table. It will soon have the look of a workshop. There are vases of flowers on each table. The families get a feeling that their child will be well taken care of in a peaceful environment.

SETTING RULES FOR DISCUSSIONS

After a few songs, I invite the families to leave if they want or need to, but make sure they understand they are welcome to come back. Most rush off to work or other responsibilities during this break. In our class, we talk right away about curriculum. For example, when we began with a block study, I asked children if they had been to the block and I named certain stores or buildings they would recognize. But, before I asked the question, I said, "Please raise your hand if you have been on the block. . . ." Or, "Raise your hand if you want to tell us something about the block." Then I call on children who have raised their hands. I compliment them for raising their hands rather than calling out. (While I love spontaneous discussions, they don't usually work well when you have large groups of young children because some kids get left out, some kids don't listen to each other, and sometimes those discussions can get loud and chaotic.) The discussion continues. We begin thinking about the upcoming block study.

ESTABLISHING PROCEDURES

In each curriculum area, *we learn the procedures as we do the work.* We do not drill until we get them right. Rather, each day I remind the children of the procedures before any transition. After a while, most children won't need the reminders. We are setting the children up to succeed.

Here is an example of how we begin Writing Workshop the first days of school. This is a routine for some children, but children who are new in the school may not know about Writing Workshop. The rules and rituals are different in each classroom, so I want to get the children accustomed to the procedures for our classroom.

> I tell the children to gather on the carpet at story circle, facing the rocking chair where I will sit. This first day, I do a mini-lesson about Writing Workshop. On a dry mark board, I draw a picture of my son playing soccer. I write a few words and then read them. Since my actual lesson is not about writing, I say, "I wrote about my son, Eric. At Writing Workshop today you can write about anything you want." I give them suggestions: family, friends, vacations, something you like to do, and so on. (In a few days, I will place a few restrictions on the choice because I really don't want them to write about TV characters.) We will introduce other topics as the year progresses. This is done very quickly, because thinking about topics is not the focus of this mini-lesson. *You should have a single focus.*
>
> My focus that day is about how to get writing folders and paper. I walk over to the boxes that contain writing folders. Color stickers on the boxes match the color of the folders. Each child has a folder with his or her name on it. This makes it easy for children to find their folder. I model (or have a child model) getting the folder. Then I

13

model going over to get paper to write on. I model returning the folder to the box after Writing Workshop. That first day, I give the children two options for types of paper with three or five lines. In the future I will introduce other types of paper, with more lines on it. I tell them they can take only one or two papers. (That's a guideline. After they use those two pages, they can get more paper.)

This first day, I give out the folders, but the children will return the folders to the boxes. The children go off to get paper and then to write. I encourage them to work very quietly, but that is not my focus for that first day. As the children work, I walk around to see the great variety of writing skills. I stoop on the floor so I will be at the level of a child with whom I stop to talk. My voice is very low.

At the end of the writing time, I give a signal ("*Ago*"). Of course, it's just the first day so I may need to quietly remind the class that they are expected to be silent after they answer "*Ame*." I ask everyone to stop work and look at me. I tell the children about how they should return their folders to the box. I ask them to clean up their work area and then come over to story circle for Share Time. Some days we won't have Share Time right at the end of Writing Workshop because we will have it at Meeting in the afternoon. Then I'll tell them to clean up their area and get in line for recess and lunch.

On the second day of school, the children will get their own folders from the boxes. We may need a quick reminder about getting our folders from the boxes. There are twenty-nine children. They need to learn to stand back and wait patiently if the area around the boxes is too crowded. I choose a child, and we do a role-play at the mini-lesson. At first I don't wait, and I pretend to push another child. The class laughs to see me doing such a terrible thing. They sense that I am joking with them. I ask them what's wrong with my behavior. They may tell me to say "excuse me," which I will do as I push. Someone will probably suggest that I should just stand and wait. We role-play and discuss this suggestion. Then, I will say, "That's a great idea. That's what we will do when it's too crowded at the boxes. We'll stand back and wait." The reasons and the new guidelines are coming from the children.

As the year goes on, I will introduce new procedures for Writing Workshop: working quietly during the silent work time, walking around the room to find words on the word walls or murals, collaborating with a friend, and so on. There are behavioral objectives as well as objectives for the development of writing skills.

WORKING COOPERATIVELY

Compliments Compliments are vitally important in our classroom community. All through the first day, I compliment children for helping each other or for working cooperatively. It's a compliment, not a thank you. "I love the way Marielle is helping Daniela. That's great."

Role-plays Another way to develop these skills is through role-plays. All through the first days of school, we do quick role-plays to show ways to work cooperatively, depending on what I observe. If I see a child grabbing all the markers, I may choose to do a marker role-play. I won't name the children who were doing the grabbing, but I may talk with them quietly afterwards.

When we read our first homemade books the second week of school (I want the children to read their homemade books together), I set up a role-play. I choose a child to be my reading partner. I whisper to him what we will be doing. I ask the partner to read the page. While he is reading, I look up at the ceiling, I play with my shoelaces, I hum, or I do anything except listen to my partner read. The children laugh. I ask them, "What's the matter?" They tell me that I'm not paying attention to my partner. I ask, "What should I do?" They tell me.

In another role-play I shout out the answers so my partner doesn't have a chance to figure out new words. The children laugh. They explain that I was shouting and didn't give my partner a chance. I ask them how I can be helpful to my partner if she doesn't know the word. I call on different children to name the ways to be helpful: encourage the partner to look at the picture, touch the first letter, sound out the word, look at the word on another page, and so on. In the process, the children are establishing the guidelines for cooperative behavior. Cooperative behavior is helping another person find strategies for reading. That way, children are learning to empower each other. Simply giving the answers doesn't really help that child in the future.

After the children have scolded me for my negative behavior, we do the role-play again. Then my partner and I do the right thing. The children and I love to laugh. Through these role-plays, we laugh as the children internalize the guidelines for cooperative behavior that we have constructed together. Using this kind of role-play has been more effective for me than simply stating lists or making charts about good behavior.

Literature In literature, there are many examples of people working cooperatively. When I see people having difficulty with cooperation, I go through the fiction in our classroom library and use that at the next read aloud. In the book talk that follows, some children will remark about the positive qualities of some characters. Some shudder at the negative. As the year progresses, I remind children of the wonderful characters from our folktales and other stories. "Wow, you are just like Blanch from *Talking Eggs*." "That's just like what Nyasha does in *Mufaro's Beautiful Daughters*. How wonderful." Before you know it, the children compliment each other using references to literature. (See Chapter 8.)

BEING SUPPORTIVE OF OTHERS

Supportive behavior is learned and this learning begins at home. For us, it begins the first days of school. Here are some examples.

Keep hands down If I call on a child, and the child does not respond, other children are quick to raise their hands or to call out the answer. First, I tell the children that I have called on _____, and they must let that person answer. They must give that person time. They must put their hands down and wait. There is no harshness or anger in my tone.

Scaffold a child who needs support Next, I must quickly try to figure out why a child I have called on is silent or is struggling to answer. If I think the child just didn't understand the question I will restate my question. I will explain my question much more carefully, thus giving the child more information. I continue to provide information or ideas so that the child can formulate an answer. Isabel Beaton calls this "scaffolding." It's important for the children to watch me help a child arrive at an answer.

Compliment supportive behavior Children in my classes learn very quickly that I love to see them be supportive of others. They constantly see me being supportive of their classmates and even family members. They constantly hear me compliment children and adults who have been supportive. All of this makes them want to be included in the process of being supportive to others. Being supportive in our class community is really cool. Many times over the years, family members have commented about how their children's behavior has changed and improved so much in this area.

Have children help other children Being supportive may mean helping a new child deal with the lunch room or recess or find the bathroom. I might say, "Who will stay with _____ at lunchtime to make him feel comfortable?" I accept all of the offers of help and compliment the children for offering to help. Or I might say, "Avery, will you help _____ find his cubby and his mailbox? It's his first day, and he doesn't know where things are in our classroom." Later, I will give Avery a compliment. Or, when a child is having a rough time at home, I may take another child to the side and say quietly, "_____ is having a problem at home. Will you please take good care of her?" If that child has had a similar problem (a divorce, a family member leaving, an illness, a death), I may tell the child whom I'm asking, unless the information is confidential. I will observe that child as she tries to be supportive, and I will quietly give suggestions or compliment what she is doing.

How Can We Enforce the Rules?

My goal is to have the children follow the guidelines we have established. I want to set the children up to behave properly (according to those guidelines), rather than let them blunder and then have to punish them. I want the children to succeed. That means they need to internalize the rules. Scolding or punishing children is unpleasant for everyone. Working for success is a mental attitude. Success is my goal.

Teaching the Expectations

Expectations are the guidelines for the rituals or the rules you have established. Expectations are the qualities of work you expect from each child (being aware of the differences in your class). I regularly remind children of my expectations.

I usually tell the children my expectations for an upcoming activity at the end of the previous activity:

> Before we enter the classroom in the morning, we stop so I can remind the children to put their homework folders in their mailboxes and give me any notes from home. I remind them to put the chairs at the tables and then get their research or interview journal.
>
> After Reading Workshop is finished, we stop while I remind children to put the books and journals away and get their folders for Writing Workshop.
>
> After Writing Workshop, I stop to tell children to put their folders away and to clean the area around them.
>
> Before recess and lunch, I often remind the children of my expectations about playing together in the yard—including other children in their games, remaining at their tables during lunch, cleaning up after themselves, and so on. Often, I remind them of being respectful and helpful to others in our class or in the school.

Let children see your joy when they meet your expectations. Let children see your joy with the way they have worked, their cooperation, their respect for each other, their singing, their drawing, and so on. Let them know how proud you are of them. Compliment (not thank) the children regularly. This is especially important when there have been improvements.

BEING BRIEF

Briefly and calmly state your expectations. There is no need to use up lots of valuable time for this. It's a statement with a period, not a question. When there are problems, review expectations or what it means to be respectful. Only when there has been a problem do I lower my voice and add a serious tone.

Approximating the Expectations

Expectations change as the year goes on and as the children become accustomed to them and internalize the rules. I expect more from a child in terms of acceptable behavior in January than I do the first week of school. The children will approximate (as Isabel Beaton says) acceptable behavior for the first part of the year, but I will expect them to follow the rules for the rest of the year (with limited reminders). That will be accomplished at a different time for each child.

As the year develops, children are expected to take charge of their own behavior. In our research groups and other classroom activities, our plays and other performances, our trips, and more, the children move from approximation to real empowerment.

The same is true for academic expectations. We use approximated spelling at Writing Workshop for a good part of first grade, but I expect that many children will write using more standard English spellings for most of their writing later in the year. For each child, the use of standard spellings will happen at a different time. The timing varies because they must first learn the many strategies we teach them for remembering or finding standard spellings in the room and because they learn standard spellings over time as they read books, signs, words on the computer, and so on.

As you gain experience teaching, you will see less and less of your time spent on discipline issues and more on academic issues. As I look at my teaching days in January, for example, my heart is joyful. I can recount all of the interesting things (academic) we did on a specific day. But, also, it feels that we have built a community in our classroom. Children are helping each other, they work better together, and there is a feeling of togetherness.

Helping Children Who Have Difficulty Following the Rules or Meeting Your Expectations

Talk quietly with any children who are having difficulty following the rules to remind them of your expectations. For example, you might quietly bring Ivan over to you or go over to him and say, "What are you supposed to do now, Ivan? What will you do if there are too many kids getting their writing folders?" Ivan should answer something like, "Stand back and wait." If he doesn't remember, I remind him of that expectation. I watch him as he gets his folder and quietly praise him when he succeeds. I may choose to praise the whole class or a bunch of children for getting their folders appropriately. "I want to compliment Hayden, Tommy, Danielle, Ivan, and Sabrina. I watched them stand back and wait when they saw it was so crowded at the writing boxes." That way, I wasn't singling out Ivan, who was so used to being singled out for inappropriate behavior at home and in school.

Complimenting Children for Meeting or Surpassing Expectations

Everyone loves a compliment. For example, if I see that only a few children are helping clean up the pencils and markers at the end of Writing Workshop, I will find those few children who are helping. I'll stop the class with a quiet "*Ago*," and say, "I want to compliment Avery, Noah, and Ebru for cleaning up after Writing Workshop. I didn't even tell them to do it. They really care about our classroom." Immediately, there will be a rush of children who will begin to clean up as we prepare to head off to lunch.

Or, after an activity or discussion, I might say, "I want to compliment the way you asked questions at that interview. It was totally amazing. Your questions were brilliant." Or, "Madeline, that was so wonderful the way you helped Sibby with her work. Boys and girls, did you see what Madeline did? She didn't do it for Sibby, but she showed her how to do it. That's so great, Madeline."

Holding Children Accountable for Their Behavior

Children must know they will be held accountable for their behavior. For example, we have a "no talking in the stairway" rule. As we enter the stairway, I usually give some signal for quiet—usually the two fingers raised in a V like the peace sign or one finger over my lips. And I look back constantly to show the children that I am watching to see that their behavior is appropriate. If I hear talking, I stop to briefly remind the children of my expectations. Then, if a child continues to talk, I stop and say, "_____, what is the rule for walking in the stairway?" They answer. "Was your behavior appropriate or inappropriate?" They answer. They know that there will be a consequence for inappropriate behavior.

Being Consistent

Rules are to be followed *all the time*. Our "no talking in the stairway" rule is always in force, not just when I feel like enforcing it. If you are not consistent, you end up wasting a lot of time dealing with misbehavior. If you enforce a rule consistently, after a while, it is internalized and stays in place. In time, the children will become silent in the stairway when they see me hold up two fingers or if I simply turn to look at them with a serious (not mean) look. In time, I don't have to do any of that, they just walk in silence.

Enforcing the Rules

Rules must be enforced. The teacher is the enforcer when children are not following the rules. You do not want to have children tattling on each other. That means you need to be watching and listening constantly.

Remember, you are trying to *prevent* inappropriate behavior and you are trying to *implement* and *enforce* the guidelines. My friend Isabel Beaton always tells her student teachers to "Scan the room." For her, that means to keep your furniture low enough so that, no matter where you are sitting or standing, you can see every child. It means that if you are working with one or two children, you look up occasionally and scan the room. The more the children have internalized the positive behavior, the more you can focus on the academic activities, and the less frequently you have to scan the room.

If you want to have a silent time during Writing Workshop, for example, then you must remind the class of this expectation and remind them to find an appropriate seat where they will not talk. If you hear the talking, you need to find the child or children involved and impose a consequence. I will ask that child, "Was that appropriate or inappropriate?" or "What is our rule about talking?" Then I ask, "What is the consequence?" In the beginning of the year, the consequence may be that a child does not get to choose where she sits that day, and I will tell her where to sit. I may give the child a brief time-out at Center Time. If the problem persists, I may tell the child that I will be meeting with his or her family. You must follow through.

In Summary

Building a community—September 13, 2001.   Teaching is building a community—a community that is safe from some of the dangers of the outside world. The day after our school reopened after the September 11 tragedy, we began class with a meeting to which I invited family members. I started by saying that I knew we had all heard about the terrible things that had happened at the World Trade Center. But, there was some good news, too. Evan's father and Grant's mother were safe. Evan's mother told about how her husband had been across the street from the Towers for a meeting. And Grant told about how his mother was late for work because she had brought him to school that day. I reassured the children that, in our classroom, we were safe.

Allison raised her hand to tell us that there was other good news. She said, "The good news is that there are more good people in the world than bad people." (Later, I posted that quote outside our classroom where it has remained to this day.) Every year I had made it my goal to create that safe space and to nurture that goodness. The last day of school, Allison's mother, Clara Hemphill, gave me this note.

> I'll never forget your calm, reassuring presence that Thursday after September 11, how we all were frightened and rattled but you made us understand that in the haven of your classroom we would be safe. I remember the tension in my shoulders relaxed and I felt somehow everything would be all right. A friend of mine whose children are nearly grown says the most important thing is to find a school that doesn't kill a

child's sense of curiosity. How wonderfully you've built on children's curiosity about the world—and taught me so much as well. . . .

Clara Hemphill, June, 2002

It's a joy being in school. It was taking a stance as a researcher that enabled me to find strategies for effective classroom management that fit the needs of my inquiry classroom. Your classroom will be different from mine, but I do hope that you will adapt some of these strategies for your classroom.

2

*Teaching the Whole Child**

Children are whole people. They are not simply people sitting eagerly waiting to learn. Children are complex. They reflect their economic and cultural backgrounds, their families, their upbringing, their biological makeup, and the society. The more we work to address children as whole people, the more effective we can be as educators.

That means we must remember that children have different styles of learning and different interests and abilities. When Howard Gardner talks about "multiple intelligences," he says, "from my perspective, the essence of the theory is to respect the many differences among people, the multiple variations in the ways that they learn, the several modes by which they can be assessed, and the almost infinite number of ways in which they can leave a mark on the world" (Armstrong 2000, v).

In my thirty-one years of teaching I've heard many teachers say things like, "I don't care what's going on at home, I'm here to teach, and that child *has* to listen to me." It's true that our aim must be to have children focus on the work and behave decently. Sometimes teachers ask in frustration, "Why can't you behave?" But often they don't reach out or take the time to find answers. Knowing more about the reasons for a child's behavior helps inform us about which strategies and techniques can enable us to be most effective working with the child. That does not mean that we must become therapists, social workers, or substitute parents. That does not mean that we must lower our standards. It may mean a quiet talk, a pat on the back, or finding ways to get the child or the family access to support or help. It may be adjusting our methods for teaching. It may mean adjusting our expectations for specific reasons.

---

*The names of children and adults in this chapter are fictitious; the situations are real.

The Democratic Right to a Quality Education

If we fail to look at the whole child, we may fail to honor the democratic right of each child to a quality education. Here are some examples from my classroom of situations similar to what most teachers have found in their classrooms. When we encounter these problems, it is our responsibility to find ways to resolve them for the benefit of the child.

Students Who Seem Unfocused But Are Listening

Some students seem as if they are not paying attention to anything that's going on. And yet, they can answer any question you ask, and they go home and tell their family everything that was said or done. Lynn surprised me constantly. She was always looking downwards as she played with her shoelaces and any tiny thing on the carpet. Lynn was sharp as could be when I asked her a question. Her parents knew just about everything that was going on in our classroom. My research and the discussions with Lynn and her family helped me understand that Lynn was listening, so I wasn't as worried when she did look down. I did work with Lynn and her parents to get her to pay attention more actively—to look at the person who was talking or to look at the dry mark board.

Students Who Seem Unfocused and Are Not Listening

There are the children who are not paying attention and/or have no idea what's going on. We need to assess the reasons for this so that we can find ways to help the child:

- Is it that our lesson is not planned well and is dull? Then we must do better. Whenever possible, lessons for young children should have hands-on activities, role-plays, or other activities. When we have interviews, I'm always thinking of role-plays, both to help children understand the information or concepts and to get active participation. The children really light up for that.
- Is it that the child doesn't speak the language that is spoken in class? We talk as a class about how to be helpful to that child. Several times, I have had a parent stay in the classroom to translate. Children offer to translate. Children try to teach the child English. We use our own sign language, pictures, and pointing at things. Children feel really good about helping. They are so delighted later in the year when the child becomes fluent and they have helped so much.
- Is it that the child is not interested in the subject matter? Then we need to find ways to engage that child because we believe that subject is important.

Sometimes that may mean a talk with the child and/or the family. Sometimes we need to work extra to make the lesson so interesting that the child will start to enjoy it. I've had this experience with a number of children during Math Workshop. We do a lot of critical thinking that evolves from hands-on work with manipulatives, the hundreds chart, and other materials. Children always come up to the front to be the teacher and explain their thinking. We go over things several times in different ways to make sure that everyone in the group understands. We don't want anyone to feel left out. It's a very active kind of learning. Soon I hear children who hadn't liked math very much laugh with joy and even call out, "I love math."

- Is it that we are teaching a subject at the wrong time of day, like having reading at the end of the school day? Well, we have to rethink our schedule. Whenever possible, the subjects that require the most focus should be scheduled earlier in the day. I like to have Center Time at the end of the day, so the children can relax after a hard day's work.

- Is it that the child is distracted by things outside of school? We need to talk privately with the child or the family to assess that. Sometimes a family doesn't even realize that their child is distracted by a problem at home. Sometimes acknowledging to the child that we are aware of the problem at home helps. Sometimes a quiet talk helps. Sometimes we need to seek outside help. We need to help a child direct his focus. Sometimes a simple reminder will help. I may say quietly, "Stephen, focus." Sometimes a quick private talk as we enter the classroom in the morning or at various points in the day will help. Sometimes the reminder that, "If you do your work, Center Time is waiting for you," can help.

- Is it that the child has problems focusing on most academic work? We need to take a closer look or get others to help us with this. Sometimes such problems can be solved by having the child sit near the teacher, work in a smaller group, or work one-to-one. Carl was a very bright child who had to sit right in the front row at story circle. In small groups he had to sit in the circle right next to the adult. We had to be very strict with him. That was the only way we could get him to stay focused.

- Is it that the child just loves to play? Perhaps the child is immature and is not quite ready for the rigors of academic work. Some children need a longer time to settle down. Some may settle down to work quite late in the school year, despite all of your efforts or the efforts of the family. There are even times when we recommend that a child remain in a grade for two years.

- Perhaps the child has learning problems, medical problems, or disabilities. They may not be able to understand what is being said or keep up with the pace of a discussion. In some situations the family and I were unaware of major hearing or vision problems, mental health, and other medical problems. As we try to understand the reasons for a child's behavior, we must be on the lookout for these kinds of problems. Sometimes we have to slow down. Sometimes we have to enlist the help of the class to help a child understand. Sometimes the whole class needs to learn to be patient.

When children have problems processing information, retaining information, sitting, focusing, and so on, you may need to get extra help. You may need to speak with the family, colleagues, an administrator, or the guidance counselor. Don't rush to have the child evaluated. Wait. Try many strategies before you recommend an evaluation. For example, Connie seemed as if she was in another world. It took a while for me to realize that she processed information very slowly. She wasn't in another world, she was right there thinking away, but she was a few minutes behind the rest of the class. It took her a few minutes to process the information and then to speak. During that time, absolutely no one was allowed to raise their hand or call out until Connie spoke. I usually had to help her with the processing and formulation of what she was going to say. I had many discussions with Connie's parents to get more background information and to think about ways to support Connie's learning. Then, I asked the speech and language teacher to do an informal evaluation of Connie. We then had a formal evaluation done so that Connie could receive special services from the speech and language teacher. When a class was formed the next year for special needs and regular education children, Connie was able to get additional support.

Students Who Focus Selectively

Some children may be unfocused during reading or math, but totally focused during read aloud or singing. Like adults, they find it easier or more interesting to learn in different areas. Yes, we have to find ways to help children succeed in every subject area. But, we should be thrilled if a child is especially focused in a particular area. Feed that interest—with compliments and encouragement, with opportunities for additional work or activities.

Children have different interests and talents. This is great. We need to plan our curriculum to meet the different interests and talents of our students. We should make every effort to make our curriculum interdisciplinary—a collage of reading, writing, math, social studies, music, drama, and science. (See Chapter 6.) That way, there is room for everyone. For example, when we do research, we may have an overall theme such as People at Work or A Special Block on Second Avenue. Within those themes, children choose their topics. For example, during a block study, children wanted to learn about vehicles, the buildings, the people who work on the block, the signs, and so on. We formed research groups based on these interests. The children asked questions. The research then focused on their questions.

As we do our research, we incorporate songs, poetry, literature, drama (plays and role-plays), science, reading, math, and writing. When children have choices and when self-interest is involved, children will be much more focused on the work. And, it can be lots of fun.

Problem Solving

Here are some examples of situations from my various classes over the years. You will be able to see the importance of working with the whole child. There are rarely simple solutions. Sometimes we have to find multiple solutions to a single problem.

Example 1—Daydreaming

A student in my class, Rona, seemed so distracted; she daydreamed much of the time. It was important for me to find out the reason(s) because she was not able to focus on her schoolwork. Sometimes during Writing Workshop or at other times during the day I found time to talk with Rona. She said she missed her daddy. At first she was afraid or perhaps embarrassed to tell me that her father was in jail. Rona yearned for him. What a relief to her when she told me. It was as if a great weight was lifted when I knew her secret. I reassured Rona that no one in the class would know about this. She could write about it or talk to me about it. I assured her that it would be private—only her mother and I would see her writing.

I arranged to speak to Rona's mother, who was already divorced from the father. Fortunately Rona's mother was willing to speak to me about this. I wanted to know what kind of contact the child had with her father, whether it would be appropriate for her to write to him, and, if so, what arrangements we should make for the mother to preview the letters. I suggested to the mother that having Rona see a therapist might be helpful. At the time the mother was working with a social worker from the prison system, so she didn't want to arrange for additional therapy for Rona. She did speak to the social worker about the letters, which Rona wrote in school. Often when I saw Rona daydreaming, I took her hand and reassured her that I loved her and cared about her. This brief hand hold and conversation enabled her to get focused on the schoolwork.

It was so sad when Rona's father did get out of jail because he didn't spend much time with her anyway. Again, I had to try to cushion the blows with a hug and conversation. That's how we made it through the year, with Rona focusing as much as possible.

Example 2—Not Listening to What the Teacher Asked Him to Do

A lively boy named Ronnie just wouldn't put the Legos away at cleanup time at the end of Center Time. I told him that he would not be able to use the Legos the next day. I just hate that kind of situation. I rarely make punishments at school that are for the next day.

I wondered what happened at Ronnie's home, so I met with Ronnie's mother, Marcy, to ask her. I asked her whether he listened when she asked him to clean up or do other tasks at home. She said, "I tell Ronnie once, then I tell him again. The third time I really mean it, and I have to scold him and threaten him." Suddenly I realized the problem. Ronnie had been programmed *not* to listen the first two times. Marcy didn't really mean it the first two times.

I explained to Marcy what she was doing. I actually explained it in programming language, which I knew she would understand. I explained that she had actually programmed him not to listen the first few times. We talked about ways to change this pattern. We decided together that Ronnie had to respond the first time, not the third time. I told her that I thought the consequence for not responding the first time should be reasonable and manageable. We talked about possibilities: loss of TV time, loss of time with his gameboy and other such toys. We talked of small ways to celebrate improvement: compliments, a trip to the movies or other low-cost special places. I assured Marcy that we would continue the dialog and that I would support her in her efforts.

Marcy sat Ronnie down to have a conversation about this. She told Ronnie that although she used to give him three chances, she would now expect him to listen and act the first time or there would be a consequence. She told him that the consequence would be a time-out from TV, which he loved so much.

Ronnie and I had a quiet talk at school about the change in his mother's expectations, and I reminded him of my expectations. I told him that his mother and I had the same rules and the same expectations, and that we would be talking to each other regularly. The consequences of this went way beyond what I had imagined for Ronnie. Not only did this new approach work, but it eliminated a lot of the fighting and tension at home. It became easier for Marcy to help Ronnie with his schoolwork and to get him to do various household chores. About two weeks later, Ronnie told me he wanted to read a *Henry and Mudge* book to me. He had read one at home. As Ronnie was a struggling reader at the time, I was about to give him the old lecture about reading books that are comfortable, books that don't have too many difficult words, when Ronnie insisted on reading any *Henry and Mudge* book I wanted him to read. I was totally shocked when Ronnie read fluently. Clearly, Ronnie had been working on various strategies for reading in our reading group and in whole class reading activities. But, it was the new situation at home and the more regular, systematic, and peaceful reading with his mother, that enabled Ronnie to make that phenomenal leap forward. Little by little, Ronnie began to listen in school the first time. I have seen such dramatic improvements many times over the years.

Example 3—Unfocused and Acting Out

Juan was difficult. He was unfocused and disruptive. I had taught his brother years before, but his brother had worked well in school. Talks and time-out's didn't work. I spoke to his mother, Sonia. I wanted to find out more about the current home situation. I asked about what happens after school when she is at work at the hospital in the afternoon and evening. She said that the older brother (a teenager) was in charge of Juan. Here was the problem. Juan's brother was not very interested in being in charge. Juan was out and about in the streets in the evening with his brother. He hung out with teenagers. The brother helped only minimally with homework. I spoke to Sonia, a single parent, about the possibility of changing her work hours. She had been on the job for many years. I knew from friends who worked at the health care workers union that it is possible to change hours when you have as much seniority as she did. I told her the name of someone from the union who would help her if she wanted to change her shift. Also, we talked about getting the older brother to get Juan to bed earlier and helping him with homework, as there was no money for babysitters.

Juan's mother did not want to change her work hours. She said she did not want to be at home with the kids. Nothing really changed at home after our discussion. I tried, but no one can solve all of the problems of our society. However, having tried was important, and it helped me find ways to help Juan in school. I knew why he was tired and restless. I knew why his homework was hardly completed.

What could I do now? I understood more about him. I was even more patient with him because the cause of the problems was totally out of our control. I spent more time helping him with schoolwork.

By the way, sometimes I have asked parents to consider changing their work hours if possible, and it has happened. It is not always possible.

Example 4—Disabled But Not Yet Diagnosed

Perhaps one of the most painful things we can go through as parents is to come to terms with our child's disability. No one wants to have a disabled child. But this is not a matter of choice. Kayla was unfocused and wiggly. Her play with others was parallel play, like that of a much younger child. She talked and sang to herself. She had no sense of the space around her, so she constantly and unintentionally bumped into other children. It was so difficult for her to make friends. Yet, she was a truly lovely, bright, and knowledgeable child. Kayla reminded me of other children I have taught over the years. I thought about how I had worked with the different families to come to terms with this. It is important to open the discussion with the family right away, to share your observations, and to get background information. It is not necessary or correct to give labels or diagnoses (ADD, ADHD, or any others), because it's not the role of a teacher to make a diagnosis. It's not usually necessary to rush to have a child evaluated. I have seen some extreme behaviors change after a few months in my class. So, I wait and observe and keep the discussions going.

At one point, though, I thought it was necessary to have Kayla evaluated. Her parents got angry with me. This, too, is a common reaction. They were aching inside. I made every effort not to be defensive and to continue the dialog and to be supportive because I know that it is difficult to come to terms with a disability. I got help from an administrator and guidance counselor. It turned out that Kayla did have a serious disability—ADHD. Once Kayla's mother came to terms with the diagnosis, she sought help right away. She joined a support group, changed Kayla's diet, and took Kayla and her brother regularly to a therapist who helped the family and who taught Kayla strategies for being in control of her life. Kayla's father had difficulty coming to terms with Kayla's diagnosis. He was not able to be supportive to Kayla's mother or to Kayla. Kayla's mother and I have become close friends. Sometimes I ask her to provide support to other families.

It was fortunate that Kayla's mother was able to come to terms with Kayla's disability. I have seen other children whose families refused to acknowledge a problem for many years. Valuable time is lost in getting help. Such children often have difficulty forming friendships, and they become isolated. And it is so difficult for the child, the class, and the teacher when a disabled child is not getting adequate help.

Over the years I have seen teachers who are very angry with parents who can't acknowledge that their child needs an evaluation or is disabled. Some teachers take out their anger on the child. That is wrong. It is not the child's fault. The child feels that antagonism and then reflects it in her behavior, which usually becomes even worse.

Yes, we all wish that it were easier for parents to come to terms with their child's problems. But, if they don't or can't, do try to understand that this is a painful thing for a parent. Keep rethinking possible approaches to that parent. Leave your anger or disappointment outside the classroom.

Example 5—Distracted and Unfocused

Susanna was having a really hard time staying focused. Every few minutes I had to remind her. I took her aside and spoke to her about what might be bothering her. After some coaxing and some reassurance that I wouldn't tell anyone in class, I found out that her mother was constantly fighting with her father. Her father was screaming and cursing, which frightened Susanna so much. She cried a lot at home when that happened. It took a lot of talk with her mother for me to uncover the problem.

I suspected that there might be some mental health problems at home. I told Susanna's mother about someone in my family who was struggling with mental health problems and how difficult that was for the whole family. If you have anyone you love who suffers from a chronic mental illness, you know what a great relief it is when someone tells you about their loved one. You share a common language, a common experience, and common problems, and you face the same stigmas from society. Untreated mental illness is a particularly difficult problem for families to face.

Now we could talk openly about the problem. We talked about ways to get the father to get help and ways to help Susanna deal with the problem. We arranged for her to see the school guidance counselor until the family could arrange something else outside of school. But, chronic mental illness doesn't just disappear, even with medication and the best of help. It is important to provide ongoing support for a child.

In the classroom, I did a lot of hand holding and talking with Susanna. I told her how difficult it must be when her mother screamed and cursed. I told her it was okay to cry when that happened, that her mother loved her but maybe couldn't help it. I told her she could talk with me or write to me when she needed to. When I saw her acting out or unfocused, I would hold her hand and try to sneak in some time in the day for a conversation.

In Summary

When we seek to teach the whole child, we are on the road to providing equal opportunity for all children. We can address their differences, their strengths and talents, and their difficulties.

3

Routines and Rituals

Having a Consistent Routine and a Schedule Is Absolutely Essential

I want our classroom to be a safe haven from the big world outside. The children should feel safe and comfortable. Whether the children's world outside of school is rushed, busy, dizzy, scary, peaceful, or stormy, I want the classroom to be calm. I want the children to know basically what to expect, to have a sense of the day ahead. If someone were to ask the children in my class what they do each day at school, they would be able to tell that person about the usual schedule we follow.

Does that mean dull and boring? *Absolutely not.* Schedules and rituals provide a shape, a structure for the day, not the content. Within the schedule and the rituals, there will be times that are fairly ordinary and times when the class will burst with excitement, where the enthusiasm builds, where you can recite poetry or sing to your heart's content. *But having a consistent routine and a schedule is absolutely essential.*

Look at the times in your own life when you have felt particularly frazzled. Often those are times when you're going through changes, and you don't know what's next. I will give the example of my own divorce over nine years ago. That miserable December and the months to follow, my life at home was topsy-turvy. All of the routines and rituals of the past twenty years were suddenly thrown into the air. However, when I entered my classroom, which I called at the time my "salvation," I suddenly felt calm and peaceful and steady. In fact, looking back at that year when I entered the classroom each morning, I closed the door on my personal life and taught fully, and it turned out to be a great year of teaching, in my opinion. (Many of the families with whom I am still in touch have told me the same.)

How could that be? I knew what to expect. *My day (not the content) was already organized for me.* We would have Research Workshop and Reading and Writing Workshop, and so on, all the way to Center Time at the end of the day. I knew

31

that a group of family members would be coming in during Research Workshop a few days a week to work on the Harriet Tubman mural, a mural done with felt on felt. (That mural still hangs in my home.) I knew at Meeting we would recite poetry and sing and have a story—all of which I totally love. I knew that during Writing Workshop it would be calm and relatively quiet and soothing for me, and that it was January of first grade and the writing coming from the children would be marvelous, so we would have lots to celebrate. I knew that at Center Time I might be working on a mural with a group of children, and we'd be chattering away as we painted. I knew that after school I would hang out in the yard and chat with family members, who were unaware at the time of what I was going through. Their friendship was so important to me. I knew that before and after school a group of colleagues at The Manhattan New School would be there for me to listen to me talk or cry—day after day.

All of that predictability gave me a sense of inner peace. I remember saying to my student teachers on those days when I walked into class after things were especially rocky at home, "Watch me today. See how I block my personal problems and try to teach fully. Watch what I do. Learn from me, because there will be difficult times in your life when you will find that your teaching is your salvation."

Does having routines and rituals mean that dealing with behavior problems, planning, or dealing with possible problems with a family member or an administrator will suddenly become easy? Of course not. But, when you have routines and rituals, at least you don't have to organize that part of the day, that part of life. That part of the day is taken care of. There's a rhythm to the day, and that rhythm is soothing to the soul of both teachers and children. Even the families feel a comfort in knowing that their child is in a calm and organized setting.

Establishing Schedules Should Be a Priority

Some schools hand teachers a schedule. Other schools allow more flexibility. The schedule at my previous school was driven by various pull-out programs, such as ESL, and special push-in reading programs that involved lots of the children. At The Manhattan New School, I create my own schedule, with the exception of the Specials (science, physical education, music, art, and computer science) and a few pull-out programs that involve small numbers of children.

The children are generally more alert and focused in the mornings, so I try to schedule reading and writing in the mornings. (See my other books *Classroom Interviews* and *The Research Workshop* for details about the schedule.) Unlike many of my colleagues, I have chosen not to have a morning Meeting. This is just my personal preference. If you are able to make your own schedule, I would suggest that with younger children, you schedule the heavily academic work earlier in the day.

Sometimes the curriculum areas don't fit neatly into the times you have scheduled or into fifty-minute blocks. How can you possibly stop a truly wonderful Research Workshop in the middle of a profound discussion or a fascinating activity? Sometimes, we don't. How can you possibly stop an exciting math activity? Sometimes, we don't. So math may run into Center Time, and Center Time will be only fifteen minutes that day. I rarely cancel Center Time altogether.

When subjects go past the allotted time, I simply say to myself, "Oh well. We'll make it up." Or "There was a lot of reading and writing during Research Workshop, so that's okay that we had less time for the formal reading activity or Writing Workshop." Because our curriculum is interdisciplinary, it's actually true that it won't hurt if one subject runs over the allotted time.

What I am *not* saying is to dispense with the schedule. *The schedule is critical.* Keeping approximately to the schedule is essential. The schedule is like the anchor for the ship. The schedule is like a pattern for making a dress. The schedule provides order to the day and the weeks and months. The schedule assures you that you will work to develop skills in all of the curriculum areas.

Does that mean you cannot make exceptions to the schedule? Of course not. You may have a trip planned, school photo day, a special event, a visitor you want the children to meet. You may find that those days when you break from the schedule are particularly exhausting because you are working much harder to maintain order and calm. The pattern of the schedule has a calming effect on the children. The pattern of the schedule and the routines actually empower the children to help run the day.

Sometimes a child starts to cry or look worried when she is uncertain about what will happen after school. She is wondering who will pick her up, where she will be going, or if she is taking the school bus. It can be unnerving to a child when plans for after school are suddenly changed. Early in the year I tell parents to send a note about any changes in their child's schedule. I collect these notes first thing in the morning so the child will feel secure that I am aware of their after-school plans. When family members forget to notify you, you may have to call their home or work so that a child won't have to worry all day.

Rituals Are a Vital Part of the Day

When we come back to the room after recess and lunch, the children put their coats in the closet and come to sit at story circle for Meeting. They know to do this because we started this ritual the first day of school. For several weeks, I reminded them to do this before we entered the classroom.

Right away, hands go up. Children want to ask for a special poem we can recite. That's because our ritual at Meeting is to recite familiar poems and learn new poems. Then we sing familiar songs and perhaps learn a new song, and then we have a read aloud and a discussion. Because of this ritual, many children look forward to Meeting. They know what will happen (not the exact content). I know that some children even lie in bed thinking about and even reciting our poems or singing our songs. They know they will have a chance to do that again the next day. Perhaps it is a ritual they will incorporate into their lives.

At Research Workshop, we do the research, and then we share some of what we have learned. This ritual makes research predictable. Also, my hope is that children will add the experience of sharing to their lives.

When we line up to go home, we have a ritual for saying good-bye. The children take their mail and then line up with their partners. We sing Woody Guthrie's song, "So Long, It's Been Good to Know Yuh." We say good-bye to every adult in the room. The adults in turn say good-bye to the children. It may sound a bit corny, but it gets children in the habit of acknowledging each other.

What Is Our Schedule?

Each morning I write the schedule on a dry mark board. At first, only a few children routinely look at the schedule when they come into the room. To get more children to look at the schedule, I refer to the schedule frequently. After Reading Workshop, for example, I may ask the children to look to see what is next. I want them to be in charge of knowing what is happening within their school day. Here is a typical schedule for our class. The parts that are in bold letters are the ones that I actually write on the board.

Our Schedule

8:40 A.M.	pick up children from the yard or lunchroom (during inclement weather)
8:55 A.M.	**Research Workshop**
9:30 A.M.	Share Time for Research Workshop
9:45 A.M.	**Reading Workshop**
10:30 A.M.	Special **(Computer Science, Art, Music, Physical Education, or Science)**
11:20 A.M.	**Writing Workshop**
12:10 P.M.	**Recess and Lunch**
1:00 P.M.	**Meeting** (poetry, singing, and a story)
1:30 P.M.	**Math Workshop**
2:00 P.M.	**Center Time**
2:40 P.M.	clean up and bus children leave
2:50 P.M.	line up for dismissal

Here is the schedule for the days we have interviews, usually once each week:

8:40 A.M.   pick up children from the yard

8:55 A.M.   begin the **interview**. The amount of time depends on the level of interest of the children.

between 9:30 and 10:00 A.M.   **Write a page for the homemade book** about the interview.

10:30 A.M.   Special **(Computer Science, Art, Music, Physical Education, or Science)**

11:20 A.M.   **Reading Workshop**

12:10 P.M.   **Recess and Lunch**

1:00 P.M.   **Meeting** (poetry, singing, and a story). If children didn't have time to finish the page for the homemade book from the morning interview, we have a shorter Meeting.

1:30 P.M.   **Math Workshop**

2:00 P.M.   **Center Time**

An urgent warning: Please don't put the blocks away! There is an increasing pressure in schools throughout the United States to focus exclusively on reading, writing, and mathematics in preparation for mandated tests. Early childhood teachers have been pressured to cut back or even eliminate Center Time, the time when children can use blocks and Legos, sand and water tables, paint and other arts and crafts materials, and more. They can do high drama in the dress-up area. Center Time is the children's opportunity to create, explore, develop critical thinking skills, and interact with classmates. It's an informal way for children to develop language skills and to work on social skills. It enables teachers to make the curriculum interdisciplinary.

Besides all of the educational value in using these materials—*it is fun.* It brings joy and laughter into the classroom. Many children don't get to play and use such materials at home in this time of TV, DVDs and videos, and busy schedules. Children love to have fun. They look forward to it. Some of the most difficult behavior problems vanish when children are free to learn using these materials. We must not banish these materials from our classrooms.

Here are a few tips if you are faced with pressure to cut out use of these materials or to eliminate Center Time.

- If you are in a position to speak up, defend your students' right to use these materials. It's best to unite with other colleagues in this effort.
- At least integrate the materials into the required content areas—for example, by painting murals about characters from literature or using blocks to make a model from your social studies theme.

- Work on improving your management skills so that you can carve out time for Center Time. Speed up transitions or time taken for lining up.
- Assess your schedule and rituals to see if there are any activities that can be eliminated.

In Summary

Having rituals and routines helps make the day predictable for students, families, and teachers. They help provide an inner peace so important in our busy world. They provide the framework for a rich curriculum and community building.

4

Family Involvement

The whole classroom community can benefit from family involvement. Family volunteers can work with individuals and groups of children. They can help with special projects or activities. They can enrich your curriculum. They bring multiple perspectives into the dialog (see my two books *Classroom Interviews: A World of Learning* and *The Research Workshop: Bringing the World into Your Classroom*). They can enable you to get to know their child better and inform your teaching. (See Chapter 2.) You and your class can enrich the lives of the families. You and your class can provide invaluable support for families. That, in turn, will benefit the children.

Family Involvement *at Home* Can Stimulate a Child's Participation in School

Family involvement can have a direct and positive impact on a child's behavior and academic work in class. When families are enthusiastic about the curriculum and activities of their children's classes in school, so many positive things happen. They talk about it at home, providing a chance for the child to review the topic and perhaps to learn even more about it from the family.

When a child sees that her family is interested, she tends to pay closer attention to the work at school, because she knows there will be more questions and discussions at home. She is excited when her family has resources (books, videos, music, news clippings, or objects) to bring to school. She is excited when her family can tell the teacher about someone to interview or when her family suggests a related trip. She is excited to add information from her family to the class discussions. All of this leads to more active and fuller participation by a child in class. *Feedback from home is a treasure.*

Involving Family Volunteers Helps with Discipline

When a family member comes for an interview, volunteers to help in the classroom, or helps with special projects, there is often a direct and positive impact on the child's behavior. The experience of volunteering helps the adult family member and the child in several ways:

- The child usually feels great pride. There are times when a child (particularly an older child) feels embarrassed by the presence of a family member. Sometimes we have to take the child aside afterwards to help him appreciate what that family member is doing for our class.
- The child usually is more focused on work while the family member is there. (There are some children who get totally unfocused when a family member is present. At times, I have had to ask that person to leave, not permanently, but until we think the child will be able to handle the situation better.)
- The child who needs individual attention will receive it. Children who are struggling with behavior or learning problems often need to work in smaller groups or alone. Volunteers can work with small groups of children, giving the teacher a chance to dedicate extra time to children who need extra help. This one-on-one time helps prevent behavior problems and addresses learning issues.
- Teachers can encourage family members to help their child develop a talent or hobby.
- Volunteers feel useful, important, and appreciated.
- Volunteering can break the feeling of isolation for people who may feel isolated at home (with babies, for example).
- Family members have an opportunity to observe how their child works in class.
- Being in the classroom or going on trips helps family members put their child in perspective. They can see their child's academic abilities in the different subject areas. They may see that their child isn't the only great reader or the only child who struggles with reading or math. They may see that their child reads fluently but tends to make up lots of words. They may see that their child is fabulous at solving math problems in her head but needs work learning how to explain that solution step by step in a journal or for classmates. They may hear their child make an incredible observation during a discussion at Research Workshop or do some brilliant critical thinking during a book talk.
- Volunteers can observe how the teacher works with their family member and with other children.

- The teacher has a greater opportunity to work with the family member so they can help their child more effectively with schoolwork or behavior.
- Teachers can help family members see that we don't judge children by their ability to read, write, or do math. Everyone is a worthy and full member of our class community and deserves the best.
- Family members can directly observe problem behaviors. They may not have believed you or understood what you meant when you told them that their child was having difficulty working with other children, that their child is mean to others, or other such behaviors. Now they may see that their child is sleepy in class or is reluctant to participate. They may observe how their child works in small groups, sits with the whole class at story circle, or plays in the block area. Then you can talk about what you are doing in school to correct problematic behaviors, and you can talk about ways to address them at home. You can work together to help the child change those behaviors. Or you can talk about the need to get outside help. *Children always correct the problems faster when families and the teacher work together.*

Family Involvement Can Enrich the Lives of the Whole Family

The comments from so many families at the end of the school year really warm my heart. In addition to talking about what the year has meant for their child, they often talk about what it has meant for their whole family. Because the families are so deeply involved in our curriculum in so many ways, they are doing and learning new things. (I am, too.) Our curriculum is not out of a textbook or a curriculum guide. It's something we create together. Our inquiry takes many twists and turns. There is input from families, children, the teacher, and others—each with different life experiences and ideas. We all gain.

Families who participate more actively become part of the class community and possibly part of the school community. This can enrich their lives.

The Teacher's *Attitude* Is Critical to Success

Your ability to involve families and to be supportive to families depends on your attitude. First, you need to believe that family involvement is important for the children. Many family members truly want to get involved with their children's classes, but so often they feel locked out. Some schools discourage their involvement. Family members can "read" you very easily. A welcoming voice and a smile can help.

The Teacher's *Behavior* Is Critical to Success

Your ability to involve families and be supportive depends on *your own behavior*. Your tone of voice and the tone of notes going home should be welcoming. You need to be friendly. When volunteers come to the classroom, they need to be given meaningful work to do. You need to make volunteers feel that they are important. You need to thank them and encourage them to come back. You, the teacher, must set the tone.

What If You Are Uncomfortable with Family Involvement in the Classroom?

Some teachers don't want family participation in the classroom. In fact, when I have led workshops on this topic, I have found that the majority of teachers were uncomfortable with family members being in the classroom other than for special events. Family members are welcome in my room at all times. There have been some who have volunteered full-time or half of every day. Others come occasionally. That's not for everybody. *Do only as much as you are comfortable doing.* If you don't know how to make family members feel welcome or you are uncomfortable with the process, please don't be afraid to try. You may want to start with family members coming in to:

- help with special projects at a specific time
- read with children at a special limited time (one hour) one or two days a week
- read to the class or sing with the class one or two times a week
- help plan a breakfast where children share their writing or a project

At first, you may want to require people to sign up in advance or limit the number of people coming at a particular time. Do what you need so that you feel comfortable and in control of your own class. Little by little you can add more.

Find Ways to Work with Family Members Who Are Difficult

This is probably the most challenging aspect of family involvement. There *are* people who are really difficult to work with. They may not like you or your way of teaching. They may not like your values. They may not like the way you work with their child. They may be mean, nasty, arrogant, or otherwise off-putting. They may have mental health problems. They may be drug or alcohol abusers. They may have problems in their lives and take it out on you. They might be very complicated people. They may seem as if they are in your room to evaluate your work or to tell the principal about what's happening in your room.

What Can You Do?

- Don't always assume that you are right. Step back and think about what the family member is saying.
- Do whatever possible to prevent yourself from getting into an argument, especially in front of the class.
- Be calm. Bite your tongue if necessary. Back off. Don't say things you might regret later.
- Ask the person to step outside the room with you to talk so you won't be talking in front of the children.
- Arrange a meeting with an administrator or guidance counselor.
- Ask colleagues for suggestions. Sometimes you will find that the previous teacher had the same problem.
- Wrack your brain for solutions. Make every effort to reach out to difficult family members.

I worked with a very difficult parent we'll call Bill. I could never criticize the behavior of his son we'll call Jim, without getting yelled at by Bill. No matter how I approached Bill, he thought I was picking on Jim. I was determined to talk about Jim's problems, but I knew I would have to take time to figure out how to approach Bill.

On a class trip, the mother said that Jim was often defiant at home. I was so glad to hear that, only because it gave me a way into a conversation. Finally, I invited both parents for a meeting. The first few minutes we talked about Jim's fabulous academic and art work. Then I said that I knew that there were problems with Jim's behavior at home and at school. I said that I wanted them to help me figure out how best to reach out to Jim. Bill offered suggestions that seemed odd to me, one of which was having a philosophical discussion about each matter. He wanted me to tell Jim how each behavior would help the world. He knew that this worked with him and was sure it would help me work with Jim. I watched the dynamic in the family as our meeting progressed. I noticed that Jim's mother, we'll call Mary, and father did not agree with each other on this. That concerned me because I saw that Jim was in a difficult situation at home. I had a better understanding of Jim. That would inform my teaching.

I told Bill and Mary that I would take time to think seriously about their suggestions. I told them that I appreciated their input. Finally, with this meeting we had opened a constructive dialog. After that, conversation was much easier. Bill got much more involved in the class. He joined us on trips and even came for an interview about his work. Near the end of school year, I was even able to suggest, without getting yelled at, that Jim get some counseling.

Perhaps the most important thing to keep in mind is not to take out your anger or frustration about family members on the child. It is not the child's fault. This is very hard for teachers, but it is vital. The child deserves a quality education—no matter what goes on at home. Make sure you are calling on the child as often as you call on others. Make sure you support his learning in every way possible.

Find Many Ways to Support Children and Families

Life can be difficult. It can be lonely. Adults raising young children often feel isolated. They may even feel that their child is the only child who is difficult at home or at school. They may feel really frustrated raising children. They may be dealing with economic problems. They may be single parents who are working and raising their children alone. They may be new in the school, the town or city, or the country.

Building a strong classroom community of children, their families, and the staff is the most powerful form of support for families. I make a conscious effort to build that community over the course of the year. I want to build bonds between the families and staff and between families. If schools can create a supportive community, it can help families weather the storms of life.

While the school doesn't have the responsibility to solve problems at home, many educators believe that helping to build support for the families of our students is very important for our children. The teacher, other school staff, community organizations, and the other families can provide support for the families. This support can enable children to have a more successful experience in your class.

Building Support for Families

Below are some of the things we do in our classroom to build support for the families:

- *first day invitation to the classroom*
  The first day of school, while we're in the school yard, I invite the families to our classroom. The family members introduce themselves and tell who their child is. I talk briefly about our curriculum, and then invite families to be my coworkers. I want them to know that I welcome their participation in the class community. We sing a few songs before the adults leave for work or their other responsibilities.
- *welcome letter*
  I send a welcome letter home the first day of school. I tell the families that they are my coworkers, and that I welcome their participation. I encourage them to get to know the other families.

- *informal talks*

  I find times to talk with family members: in the school yard before and after school, during my preparation time when the children are at Specials, on the phone, at a restaurant at lunchtime. I make every effort to talk with family members. We talk about their child, the class, or school, as well as our lives and the world around us, which is different with every family. I make every effort to link families together. For example, when I am talking with a parent in the school yard, I introduce her to other parents, relatives, or babysitters. Quite often, friendships evolve from these introductions.

- *notices home*

  I encourage families to get together. I do this in our Family Homework or in letters home. For example, I may suggest that children work on a project together, that families go to a museum, zoo, or library together, or that families go to an event together. I suggest they go to the home of a classmate who has a computer so they can do their research.

- *class meetings*

  MNS has a Curriculum Night early in the school year. Some teachers plan additional family meetings. After we discuss curriculum issues, I always leave time for questions and discussions. So often, these meetings run much longer than the allotted time because we talk about problems and concerns. Being flexible and allowing for that extra discussion is very important (as long as people feel free to leave when they need to).

- *family-teacher conferences*

  Our school has two formal conferences each year. The focus of these conferences is about the child's academic and social development. When I see the need, I will discuss parenting issues such as helping with schoolwork or establishing routines at home for homework, discipline, bedtime. Often, I draw from my own experience as a parent or from my prior experience with other families. Please note, I never pretend to be a social worker or a therapist. For some problems, I will recommend that a family get help through the school or outside agencies. We may schedule additional meetings for follow-up. Family-teacher conferences are always confidential unless a family wants me to discuss a particular problem openly.

- *family homework*

  This is our main vehicle for keeping families informed about our curriculum, about issues to discuss with their child, about class and school activities, and about ways they can help at home and in the classroom. The children receive the Family Homework packet on Mondays, and there are two pages of homework assignments they must return on Fridays. The reading and math worksheets are directly related to the concepts we are working on in class. There is always extra credit, which is voluntary, for those families who want to or have time to extend the learning even further.

My intention in the Family Homework is to get families to spend meaningful time together and to strengthen their bonds. Because the families learn about the curriculum, the people we have interviewed, the research we are doing, they are able to have more meaningful discussions with their children about school. They can talk about Bobby, the sanitation worker, Tommy's father, Nick a building superintendent, or Zori, who was a child laborer. They can make their own hundreds chart and marvel at the patterns. They can look for cornices, lintels, sills, and gargoyles on the buildings as they go out for a walk. They may take up the suggestion to boil water to see how steam is made in a boiler, or beat the heavy cream until it turns to butter.

My intention in the Family Homework is to have the families become my coworkers. There is such power in having the families serve as teachers. In so many areas, families know far more than an individual teacher or a book. When we are doing research about the old days, I asked the families to have their children interview them or elderly relatives, neighbors, or friends. When we were doing research about different cultures, the families were primary sources of information.

Developing the Family Homework each week is a lot of work. I do it at home during the weekend because I need to take a lot of time. Other teachers do homework packets in school. The critical thing about the homework is that we use it to promote family involvement in the children's education. This kind of homework helps create a wonderful environment for learning, parenting, and teaching.

- *family involvement in class activities*
The first day of school I send home a paper asking families how they want to volunteer to help our class in school or from home. They can sign up to: help in the classroom, arrange or go on trips, or print our homemade books. They can help us with music, science, art, cooking, dance, storytelling, and so on. There is another sign-up sheet so that family members can participate in our social studies research. For example, they may sign up to come for an interview or find someone to interview about a particular topic. They can send in books, videos, newspaper articles, and other resources.

All through the year, I put suggestions in the Family Homework so that families can get involved. For example, if we are doing research about paleontologists, the Family Homework might ask family members to save and clean bones from the chicken, pig, sheep, or cow meat they had for supper. I might ask if they would help us contact Woody Guthrie's daughter for a

44

study of Woody Guthrie or arrange an interview at the local grocery store for a block study.

The teacher and family members get a chance to talk. The teacher and children learn from family members in so many ways. Family members feel so good when they have helped our class. Also, children get to feel comfortable with the other class family members. Be sure to thank people for their participation.

- *language bulletin board*
  The Manhattan New School has a bulletin board of languages spoken at our school. It lists the language and the children who speak that language. We use that (and informal discussions among teachers) to link families together for translation and support.

- *special meetings*
  When the need arises, I arrange for meetings with a school guidance counselor, a social worker, a parent educator, or others who will work with individual parents or with a group.

- *phone calls*
  For family members who can't get to the school because of other obligations, we talk on the phone. Also, our class parents make calls to the families about special events.

- *schoolwide events*
  The Manhattan New School has a Parent Teacher Association that sponsors grade-level parties, a school picnic, an international dinner, a talent show, a street fair, book fairs, ice-skating parties, a picnic in Central Park, and other events. Some of these are fund-raising events. Also we have a parent-teacher leadership committee that plans parent classes in writing, parenting, and so on. Family members and staff spend many hours planning and working together to make these events a success. Many friendships evolve from these activities.

- *phone directories*
  The Manhattan New School has a schoolwide phone directory. Families give written permission to have their phone number and address listed. Individual classes have their own class lists compiled by parents. This gives families easy access to each other. When there are divorces or complicated situations, I am very careful to let the custodial parent decide how the family should be listed. Sometimes only one parent or family member is listed and sometimes two parents and their separate phone numbers are listed.

- *special events for our class*
  We plan events for our class that will involve the families. We have special breakfasts that begin first thing in the school day so adults can hurry off to

work or other responsibilities. We have also had luncheons and some evening events. Other classes at MNS schedule events at various times, including events to share children's writing, social studies research, and literature, or good-bye parties for student teachers or other adults. My preference is to have these events the first thing in the morning or in the evening, to maximize the participation of family members. You can read below about our biggest events, the Family Celebrations.

The great thing about these events is that the adults get to meet each other and talk. Often I see them looking for a piece of paper and exchanging phone numbers. I see families making arrangements for playdates, sleepovers, babysitting, and so on.

What Is Our Family Celebration?

Our class has two Family Celebrations, usually in late November or early December and late May or early June. These events take place from 5:30 to 7:30 P.M. We celebrate our learning and our community. Children sing, recite poetry, and may perform a play. This is followed by a potluck dinner. Here are a few tips for making this a successful event:

- Set the date as much in advance as possible so families can arrange to be there.
- Plan it as an evening event to maximize participation.
- Announce the date over and over in Family Homework and in letters.
- Make an invitation families can give to friends, relatives, and babysitters.
- Send a notice home several weeks in advance asking people to sign up for the setup and cleanup committees and to let you know which food they will bring for the potluck. Keep a list of the foods, so you know whether you will have enough main dishes, salads, and desserts. You may have to ask a few people to change what they are bringing so you don't end up having too many of one type of item.
- Ask class parents or other family members to call all of the families to remind them.
- Make special arrangements to be sure all children are at the Celebration. If parents can't go or can't get the children there on time, other families may take the children. In some cases, I have agreed to take care of the children at school until the families can get there.
- Invite your colleagues.
- Invite people who have helped your class in any way. We invite everyone we have interviewed as well as people who have helped in other ways.
- Thank people for their help.

While the November celebration is a lovely event, many families are just getting to know each other, and our classroom community is in its early stages of growth. The May or June celebration is a joyous event. Our children and class families have worked together on our daily activities and on special projects. This has made us a strong community—both in school and among families. You can see it in the smiles, the hugs, and the tears.

Special Problems

Family Members Who Feel That Their Child Is the Only One Who's Difficult at Home

I love my students. As one of twenty-eight or more children in class, they are often so anxious to please the teachers. They are often so lovely and well behaved. Sometimes when I tell a mother that her child was wonderful in class, she is shocked. She wonders how that could be when her child talks back to her and is so disrespectful at home. Doing homework with her child is like fighting a civil war. Getting her child to go to bed at a reasonable time is a major battle. Life can get miserable. She can feel incompetent.

It's important that parents or caregivers know that this is typical behavior for young children at home. They can get defiant, mean, and really hurtful. How many parents have felt the pain of hearing their young child say to them, "I hate you." Usually, this testing of one's parents continues and takes many forms as children grow older. With the oldest or an only child, parents will usually be surprised to hear that this behavior is typical. Introduce them to other parents who will confirm this. Learning that you are not the only person with this problem is comforting. It helps you realize that you are not a "bad" parent.

Sometimes talking with an individual family member is useful. We talk about strategies for dealing with their child. I assure them they are not alone. Sometimes we take time at Curriculum Night to discuss such issues. For example, if a mother complains that her child just won't cooperate when he is doing homework, we will discuss this. I will ask, "Is there anyone else here who has trouble getting their child to do homework?" I may even say it with a little laughter in my voice, because I know it's a big problem for many families. Then, there will be an outpouring of comments such as,

> My child takes three hours to do the homework that should take only a little while.
> My child is always fighting with me when we do the homework.
> My child gets really mean to me when I try to help with schoolwork.

People call out, "Me, too." There is laughter when people realize this is a common problem and they are not alone. There is an exchange of ideas of how to deal with this. There is comfort in shared misery. Families with older children may have been through this already and can give other families hope. Over the years I have seen many people break through that feeling of isolation when they hear others talking about having similar problems such as problems with homework, bedtime, getting children to listen to them, and so on. Sometimes that portion of the meeting has the feeling of a support group.

Family Members with Mental Health Problems

Many teachers aren't aware of the symptoms of chronic mental illnesses, such as schizophrenia, bipolar disorder, chronic depression, and so on. Sometimes you hear teachers talking about parents who are "crazy" or "insane" because of things they have done or said. These words are inappropriate and serve only to stigmatize people with mental illness. If you observe behavior that leads you to suspect that there may be mental health problems at home, problems that interfere with parenting, or problems that may harm a child, do your research. Read up about mental illness. Talk with the guidance counselor and administrators both to learn more and to think about whether or how to intervene. You might decide to:

- Arrange a meeting with someone from the family and the guidance counselor or social worker.
- Speak with a family member about the problem. Often, that isn't possible. If it is, then it may be possible to refer the family to a support group or another source of help.
- Change your attitude about that family member. Rather than see him as "crazy," remember that some of the inappropriate behaviors are symptoms of the illness. Do not be angry with him. That may prevent the communication you need.
- If you, your principal, or the guidance counselor can't approach the family about getting help for the adult, try to form a safety net for the child in school. Find a volunteer who will spend extra time with the child, perhaps helping her with schoolwork or working on a special project.

Family Members with Alcohol or Substance Abuse Problems

These problems always have an impact on the whole family. If at all possible, you or a guidance counselor needs to talk with an adult in the family to urge them to seek help. Your guidance counselor or administration may be able to refer them to help. It is important that the child also be referred to a family support group. If the family will not seek help, try to form a safety net for the child in school. Inform yourself by reading books or articles about this issue.

If you and/or your administration thinks the child is in any danger or is suffering from neglect, it is your legal (and I believe moral) responsibility to report that to the proper town, city, or county agency. You must protect the child.

Families in Crisis

Your class families may be dealing with very serious situations: illness, death, loved ones moving away, sudden need to care for relatives, loss of jobs, separation, and divorce. Your concern and caring about family crises is a very important source of support. It is so helpful for the family to know that you are there for their child during this difficult time.

- Let families know early on in the year that these situations are important for the teacher to know about so that you can be supportive to their child.
- Make hospital visits and home visits and attend funerals. Be there for the family.
- In cases of separation and divorce, try to arrange ongoing meetings with one or both family members. Send home two copies of notices.
- When appropriate, refer families to relevant support groups.
- Let the family know what you are doing in class to provide support for their child. This is so comforting to the family.
- When appropriate, read relevant stories or poems to the class or recommend or send books home to a family.

Families Who Need Ways to Get Help with Schoolwork

There may be a number of reasons a family cannot or does not help their child with schoolwork. Perhaps a family does not speak English. Perhaps the parents or guardians are not literate. Some adults are not available to help their children during the evening. They may be working more than one job. They may get home too late or are too exhausted to help. We should make every effort to get those families involved in their children's education. Here are some suggestions:

- If the adults work at night, I encourage them to work with their child during the weekend and even let the child turn the homework in on Mondays instead of Fridays.
- If the family doesn't speak English, I can link them with a family that speaks the same language.

- If many of the families do not speak English fluently, I speak to other families or announce in our Family Homework that I need families to volunteer to help other families with the homework.
- For families that do not speak English, I arrange to have the homework or letters home translated, either orally or in writing.

In Summary

Doesn't this sound like a lot of extra work for teachers? It is. It's certainly not in our job description. But, if we view education as more than filling children with information for the test, and if we see the importance of family involvement, we will be committing ourselves to that extra work.

Dear Paula,

You have given our children so much this year. You have inspired them to learn, write, and more importantly, to become socially conscious, caring people. We have seen you put everything you have into this class and constantly give above and beyond what is expected of a teacher. You have become a part of all of our lives, and we appreciate everything you have done for our children.

From the families and children of 1-407, June 2002

5

Classroom Management—
Tips from an Old-Timer

The first part of this chapter describes basic management issues. Every classroom is different. Each teacher has a different personality and different constraints imposed by a particular school or school system. The practices in this chapter are ones that work for me, practices that have evolved during my thirty-one years of teaching. I sincerely hope you will be able to adapt some of them for your classroom, as I know they will help you dedicate more time to curriculum.

- acting as if you are in charge
- teacher or friend?
- responsibilities
- consequences
- signals for getting kids' attention
- instructions
- pleasant ways to get children to do what they are told
- transitions
- class discussions
- room setup
- placement of materials
- workplaces
- getting in line
- preparing for lunch and recess
- dealing with lunch and recess
- dealing with recess on snowy or rainy days
- calming down after lunch and recess
- the bathroom
- cleanup

In the second part of this chapter, I talk about problem situations.

- solving problems
- working with a child who won't listen
- working with a child you don't particularly like
- working when you're tired
- working when you're upset
- dealing with Monday mornings or the day after vacations
- dealing with children before holidays or vacations
- dealing with tired children
- dealing with administrators
- ending the school year gracefully

Part 1: Basic Management

Acting as If You Are in Charge

YOUR TONE OF VOICE IS IMPORTANT

When you're trying to get children to do something, *do not ask questions.* Parents and teachers make this mistake all the time. Parents say, "It's time for bed now, honey, okay?" Of course it's not okay. When children are in a quiet line for lunch, teachers often ask, "Are you ready now?" Then, children start talking again as they answer the question.

MAKE A STATEMENT

Put a period at the end of your sentence. Your voice should go down at the end of the sentence, not up (as in question mode). "No talking." "Stand silently in line." "The talking must stop. It's time to do your writing." "Hitting is absolutely unacceptable." Use a serious, but not a harsh or mean, tone.

STUDY YOUR OWN BEHAVIOR

Do you tend to ask questions when you give directives? If so, practice giving directives in sentences that end with a period.

BODY LANGUAGE IS CRITICAL

You can say anything you want, in the most calm, low, or firm voice, but, if your body doesn't deliver the same message as your words, children just don't believe you. Sit up or stand up straight, rather than in a casual position. Use your eyes. Look at a child or look the class in the eyes. Stare. Practice in the mirror. Practice on family or friends. Be serious. Look serious (not mean). Smiling is usually not in order when you're trying to get a child to improve her behavior. There's plenty of time for smiling when things are going well.

There are some exceptions to the smiling rule. There are some children who lock themselves into an angry, battlelike mode. You may find that your sternness and strictness make them dig in deeper and deeper. In that case, humor can work. I may make a (fake) angry face and say to that child, "Rena, if you don't stop that fooling around (or whatever the negative behavior), I'm going to send you to the moon." The other children usually laugh and say things like, "Oh yeah, Paula, sure!" Suddenly the child will break into a smile, and you are then able to discuss the problem in a calm and reasonable way. It does work. Use this technique sparingly because you don't want to play games every time you want a child to listen.

Teacher or Friend?

Student teachers and newer teachers have such difficulty with the teacher or friend question. I had the same problem when I was a new teacher. I wanted the children to love me. I couldn't bear using that stern voice or giving a time-out to children. That's a natural way to feel.

You are the teacher. You must establish your authority. If you're there to be loved, you're making the fatal mistake of trying to please the children and families rather than doing what is in their best interest. You simply cannot be effective as a teacher if you are so worried about being a friend that you cannot establish and maintain a calm and orderly classroom.

If children are constantly calling out, doing whatever they please, or being disrespectful to other children and to you, you can't teach, because too much time is spent calling the class to order and disciplining children who are misbehaving. I remember wondering during my first year of teaching when I would ever find time to actually teach, because I felt that a huge percentage of my time was spent on classroom management. Wanting to be loved and lacking strategies were my biggest problems.

We cannot worry if the child or the family loves us. However, if you are able to manage the class well, the children are deeply involved in the learning, and you have a strong curriculum, they are bound to love and respect you. Our goal should be to establish a good working relationship.

Families usually say they love having their children in my class. But once, I had a student in my class whose parents wanted her to be removed from my class because she often had some time-out at Center Time. I was heartbroken. The child was wild, undisciplined, and disrespectful when she entered my class. She had been the same in kindergarten where she had a new teacher. The parents felt that having a consequence such as a few minutes of time-out was bad for the child's mental health. I believed that lack of consequences at home was a large part of the problem, although I did not say that during the discussion at the principal's office. The principal agreed with me about this. Together we explained why there were consequences for negative behavior, and we assured the family that little by little we would all see an improvement in the child's behavior. It is rare that a child is removed from a class in our school, so the child remained. I continued to impose consequences for the child's rudeness, pushing others, and other inappropriate behavior. Sometimes the child had to sit at Center Time to write a letter of apology to someone she injured, sometimes I met with her, and sometimes I had her sit and think for a while about what she had done. Sometimes she had to complete her work.

I continued to communicate with the parents even though I felt so badly. I tried to step back and not take it so personally. We met again without the principal and took a closer look at the child's behavior at home and how the family dealt with her. They treated her as if she were a friend, not a daughter. They were finally able to admit to themselves that their child had no limits placed on her at home, and that she was practically in charge of the adults. I urged them to take steps to place themselves in charge, to have rules with consequences, and to enforce those rules. I urged them to follow up at home with problems from school. We even agreed on what the consequences might be: take away TV time, impose time-out from a favorite activity, and so on. There was a marked improvement in the child's behavior, to the point that it became a pleasure watching her function in the class. Her joy showed in her smile.

Responsibilities

Our goal is to have children be responsible for their own behavior within the rules and procedures that have been discussed previously. Early in the year I tell the children that they are responsible for their own behavior. For example, when a child is not acting in a responsible way, I say, "You are responsible for sitting the appropriate way so people behind you can see. It's your responsibility to tell yourself what to do. That isn't my job. It's yours."

For most curriculum areas, children can decide for themselves where to sit. When I see that some children have made poor choices about where to sit for an activity, I remind them at the beginning of that activity to "Think about where you are sitting. If you are sitting next to someone you know you are going to talk to, do the smart thing." They may decide to stay where they are and be quiet. Or they may find another seat.

All through the school year, you will hear me say things such as:

Be your own teacher. Tell yourself what to do.
Be in charge of your own behavior. That is not my responsibility. It's yours.
You're in charge of telling yourself how to _____.

Be your own teacher. Please take that job away from me. I'm going on vacation. (We laugh.)

Wow, you took that job away from me. That's great. Now, I'm going on vacation. Yeah! (We laugh.)

Consequences

Another way to think about discipline is to look at how we program children's behavior. Think about how toddlers learn the rules and expectations of the adult family members. If a toddler wants something, and she cries and whines enough, her parents may give it to her just to avoid further conflict. The child then realizes that after only a few tries, crying and whining work. The child has been programmed to know that the rules really aren't rules because they can be broken easily by acting in a certain way.

Instead of letting the child violate or constantly negotiate the rules, parents need to enforce the rules. The first time, the parent needs to tell the child that crying, whining, or hitting will not get them what they want. That is the consequence. The adults must continue this policy, even if the child cries or whines. In time, children will get the message and will stop the crying. Adults need to help children develop positive strategies for getting what they want or for solving problems. Little by little children will approximate these positive strategies.

The process for problem solving in the classroom is similar. Initially, we discuss guidelines and rules for behavior. These rules are now called expectations. We repeat the expectations over and over in the beginning of the school year and as needed during the rest of the year to prevent rules from being broken or ignored. The children are approximating following the rules. As they do that, it's important for the teacher to compliment (not thank) them. "I just love the way you stood back and waited for the other children to get their writing folders. That is so responsible." After a while, following certain rules is just routine, and you can save your compliments for other things.

When the rules are followed there are positive consequences:

- There are compliments to the child and the family.
- Children, teachers, and family members feel proud.
- There's a lot of learning going on and the whole community can get joy from that.
- The work itself can be lots of fun.
- Children get to make choices.
- Children get to have Center Time, which is a lot of fun.
- The children's positive behavior is noted on the assessment reports.

As we implement the rules, we must have consequences if the rules are broken. Some children observe what happens to their classmates, and they may choose not to test you. Other children will continue to test you and the rules until the point that they realize it is useless and unproductive to keep testing. When they finally realize that the rules are for everyone, and they are meant to be followed, they will ease up. By then, they have internalized the rules and expectations, and they take responsibility for enforcing the rules for themselves. That will happen only if you enforce the rules and guidelines with consequences.

We don't change the rules in our classroom unless I realize that a rule is not a good one. Sometimes you'll hear me say to a child in April, "This is the same rule we have had since the first day of school. Our rule hasn't changed."

Yes, consequences for inappropriate behavior are necessary, but *every effort should be made to prevent inappropriate behavior* and thus eliminate the need for negative consequences. It's important for new teachers to look at the official rules (state, city, town, school) about corporal punishment, as there may be things you thought were legal, but are not. Hitting is illegal. Putting children in the corner with their back to the class and putting children in the hallway as a punishment are illegal in many states. We still see children out in the hall alone for punishment in schools all over the world. While I can understand why teachers may want to send disruptive children to the hall, it can be demeaning and counterproductive.

Gregory was one of the most difficult children I have worked with. The previous teacher sent Gregory and a paraprofessional out to the hallway to work every time Gregory misbehaved. He knew how to get sent out of the room—just misbehave. And he expected to be rejected constantly. It was demoralizing for him. He felt rejected and unwelcome during a time he was adjusting to major changes in his personal life. When he came to our class the next year, Gregory expected to be sent out to the hallway the first time he misbehaved. That didn't happen. As difficult as it was to keep him inside the room, I refused to send him out because I didn't want him to feel rejected. We had to surround him with love and support. We had to teach him about love and friendship and cooperation. It wasn't easy. But, with a mix of that love, support, consistency, and compliments for positive behavior and consequences (such as time-out at Center Time, which he loved so much) for inappropriate behavior, Gregory made tremendous progress.

CONSEQUENCES MUST MEET THE INFRACTION
When children's behavior is inappropriate, we have consequences. There are different consequences for different situations. *Do not threaten consequences you know you can't enforce.* For example, you shouldn't say, "You can't go on the trip," when you know that everyone is going. You shouldn't say, "You can't be in the class

play," when you know that it is very important that everyone be in the play. You shouldn't warn, "I'm going to send you to the principal's office," when the principal may not be there or may not want the child to be there. After a while, children will know that these are empty threats or warnings.

Choose smaller consequences and be consistent about enforcement. For some children, missing a few minutes of recess or Center Time is enough to bring about a change in behavior. For others, additional consequences are needed. For example, when a child has continuing problems with his behavior in line, he has to either be my partner or stand near the front of the line. If a child continues to talk during a silent work time, he will get a brief time-out later in the day at Center Time. You may want to develop a list of consequences you think are appropriate for your situation.

Here are some consequences we use in our class:

- time-out from recess. Sometimes I will ask the school aides to bench a child for a portion of or all of recess (depending on the problem).
- time-out from Center Time (never an academic activity). Children who fool around or are not working during a work time must make that work up during Center Time. As soon as the work is completed, a child can have Center Time. (This is not meant for a child who has been working hard but has not finished.)
- sitting in a spot for a specific time. A child will sit at a table and watch the lesson from there rather than sit with the rest of the class. I want to be sure that the child can see and hear the lesson.
- a quiet talk with the teacher to discuss the problem and find solutions
- temporary removal of choices—where to sit, who will be the line partner, where to stand in line, and even which research group to be in. I may send the child to another spot in the room, either to another table or on the carpet. The child may need to sit near an adult or away from a particular child.
- an apology (oral or in writing)
- a letter home (written by the child or the teacher)
- a phone call from the teacher to the home
- a meeting of the teacher with a family member

A child can earn her rights back if she takes responsibility for her behavior. It's very important that children not feel permanently locked out of decision making.

When a child repeats the inappropriate behavior too many times, I have a quiet talk and ask him if he wants to resolve the problem with me or if we should get his family involved. I usually give him the option first of resolving it without his family. If the problem continues, I will involve the family.

Signals for Getting Kids' Attention

You need signals to get children to be silent, but silent for a purpose. When I use a signal, I expect children to be silent, to stop their work or other activity, to look at me, and to listen. I may want to let them know that Writing Workshop is over, that I want them to lower their voices during Center Time, that there is someone we have to listen to on the loud speaker, that it's time to line up for recess, that I want to share someone's breakthrough or terrific writing, and so on.

In Chapter 1, I describe how I came to love the Swahili signal, "*Ago*," "I want your attention," and the response, "*Ame*," "I am listening." Sometimes I say "Excuse me," which the children learn also means, "Stop doing what you are doing and listen." If I have asked the children to talk with the child who is next to him, I give them a few minutes to talk, and then I say, "Stop."

Signals I will never use include: "shhhhh" or "shut up." I have observed teachers who say "shhhh," and it seems that they have to say it constantly. The "shhhh" signal doesn't have a specific meaning, therefore it gets perhaps only a momentary response. "Shut up" is rude. I don't use lights off or bells. For me, they are too labor intensive. I want a signal that doesn't require me to move or to get a piece of equipment.

In this society we are barraged with noises. There are lots of ways to reduce noise in our school. Signals can also be nonverbal. A peace sign of a V means silence. One finger covering my lips is a reminder on the steps or in the hall that there's no talking. Staring at a child's pencil can get him to put it down. Motioning with one's hand can get children to follow in the line or to stand up. A nod of the head can mean yes or no.

The lower your voice is when you communicate, the lower the children's voices will be. Start the first day with the calm low voice. Remind yourself, especially in times of stress, that your voice should remain low and calm. If you do that and use the nonverbal signals, your classroom will eventually feel peaceful. Then sounds will come from the excitement of learning.

At a faculty meeting when Shelley Harwayne was the principal of our school, we went around the room to tell what signals we each used to get the children's attention. It was great. It's a matter of choosing the signals that work best for you and your class. You can read about various MNS signals in Shelley Harwayne's book *Going Public, Priorities and Practices at The Manhattan New School* (1999, 122–23). Other suggestions can be found in *Classroom Management for Elementary Teachers* (2000, 114–15), by Carolyn Evertson, Edmund Emmer, and Murray Worsham. Also, ask other teachers.

Signals are meant to illicit a particular behavior. The first day of school, I introduce our signals and their meanings. At first, children approximate the expected behavior. In the beginning, I provide extra reminders. After a few days, I inform the children that they must follow the signal, and that there will be a consequence if they do not follow the signal. When I see children ignoring the signal, I do impose a consequence. The consequence may be a discussion with me or a very brief time-out from Center Time.

Instructions

It's essential that you're very clear about what you want children to do. You can usually tell when you've blundered by looking at the expressions on children's faces or watching them. Do they seem puzzled about what to do? Are they milling around? Our aim in giving instructions is to have all the children understand so they can implement them. We want to *prevent* problems. Here are some suggestions:

- All work and movement should stop while you give instructions. Unless there is an emergency, do not shout instructions so they can be heard over the talking in the room. This just increases the amount of noise in the room. It is not effective. Use a signal (*Ago*, clapping, or whatever signal works for you), wait for the silence and for the movement to stop. You may need to use the signal a second time. Wait for silence. Only then should you give the instructions.
- Give instructions clearly. "Turn to page four." "Get in line." "Talk with your partner about. . . ."
- If there is more than one step, give directions slowly and step by step. "I want you to put your reading journal away, clean up the area where you were working, get your lunch box and jacket, and then get in line for lunch." "I want you to turn to page six in our homemade book and look for the words that begin with th as in *throw*. Circle those words."
- Look around as you give directions. If everyone seems to be listening and understanding, you don't need to repeat them. If there are children who don't seem to be listening carefully or who have difficulty following directions, there are a few things you can do:
  Repeat the directions.
  Change your wording to make it clearer.
  Call on a child to repeat the directions.
  Call on a few children to repeat the steps if the directions are complex. (Don't act angry, you are just trying to clarify any confusion or get a child to do the right thing.)
- If you think there may be children who don't understand, ask, "Is there anyone who is not sure what you are supposed to do?"

- If a child doesn't follow instructions, deal with him privately, if possible. Call him over to you, or go over to him, and ask him to repeat the instructions. If a child is unable to follow directions, you may want to help him yourself or get another adult or a child to help. If a child seems to be deliberately not following directions, you may want to ask him why, or just ask him whether his behavior was appropriate or inappropriate. If he acknowledges that it was inappropriate, tell him to get busy doing the right thing. If this is a constant problem, ask the child, "What happens when your behavior is inappropriate?" If the child answers, "I get a time-out," tell him "Yes, you do." It's important that children know the consequence of repeated inappropriate behavior.

Pleasant Ways to Get Children to Do What They Are Told

SINGING COMPLIMENTS

Did you know that singing really works? When I want more children to help with cleanup, or I want children to get in line faster, I often make up a song about it. The song praises those who are doing the right thing. For example, I may sing to the tune of "All Around the Mulberry Bush," "I like the way that Allison is helping, I like the way that Tommy is helping, I like the way that Garrett is helping, yes, I do." Suddenly I will see lots of other children helping with the cleanup—just because they want to hear their name in my song. Or, "I like the way Chandra and Hayden are in line, I like the way Danielle and Lena are in line, I like the way Emma and Rani are in line, yes I do." Suddenly, the line takes shape, and I gradually add names of line partners to the song. Or, "I like the way that Emmy is helping, she's making our room so nice and clean, she's picking up pencils from the floor, that's so wonderful."

I make up all sorts of songs using all sorts of familiar tunes. They are not brilliant pieces of music. They are kind of silly. They are just compliments. They work magic, and they sure are more pleasant than the sound of scolding. It's a really useful way to get things going in a positive direction when things seem a bit messy or chaotic.

SPOKEN COMPLIMENTS

Another method is the spoken compliment. For example, when I want more children to get involved in the cleanup, I stop the cleanup with a signal. Then I compliment the children who are helping. It's a compliment, not a thank you. The other children usually rush to help after that.

Transitions

Transition time is when children are going from one activity to another. Before the transition, I always tell the children what they are expected to do. They may be putting things away, getting journals or folders, finding a seat, getting in line, and so on. *No one, absolutely no one may walk around, continue working, or talk while these instructions are being given. I never give directions while children are talking, playing with math manipulatives, tapping, or doing other such activities.*

During the transition, the room is filled with movement and talking. That's fine. Children need that time to walk around, to stretch, to talk with each other, to go to the bathroom, or to relax. Within a few minutes most children settle down and get ready to start the next activity. After the three- to five-minute transition, I give a signal, and we get started. That's when work begins again. Or, if the children are in line, after the signal, they must be silent. When there's a transition into Writing Workshop, for example, after about five minutes, I say, "*Ago,*" and the children respond "*Ame,*" and there is silence. I announce that it's time to work in silence unless you are working with an adult or you are collaborating on some writing with another child.

It's important that we take time to assess what is happening in our classrooms. If something doesn't seem to be working well, it's time to look for solutions. For example, after months of allowing talking during the whole Writing Workshop, I realized that relatively little writing was going on. That's why we now work in silence unless children have permission to collaborate.

Often, we have time near the end of Writing Workshop when children can talk quietly with others. During the transition to Reading Workshop when we work in small groups, the children get their journals and a pencil, open their journals to a blank page, return books from their book baggies, select new books (from designated boxes) for their book baggies, and read to themselves. I introduce these procedures in the beginning of the year. Before that transition, I do remind the children about the journal and the book baggies, because there are usually several children who need reminders.

Class Discussions

We have many different types of discussions:

- discussions around a role-play
- discussions about literature
- discussions about supporting other children
- discussions about our research, interviews, and trips
- discussions about behavior
- discussions about the world around us

For any activity in your classroom, you need to ask yourself, "What is the purpose of this activity?" While discussions may have different focuses, my main goals are the same:

- gather information
- further children's and your understanding about the topic
- promote critical thinking
- work on skills (reading, writing, math, social studies, science)
- share thoughts and opinions
- encourage participation by children who seem uninvolved
- develop listening skills
- involve all of the children

If you observe class or group discussions in classrooms around the world, you will see a sad pattern. The teacher sets the topic or asks the questions and then calls on a few children to answer. The teacher usually calls on the same children who either think quickly or get their hands up quickly. That means that most of the children don't participate actively. Here are some rituals we have created to promote more democratic and active participation.

TALK WITH A PARTNER

Often I say, "Talk with the person next to you about. . . ." When we do this, all children will get a chance to speak and be heard. It does require work by the teacher; however, because there will always be children who, for whatever reason, don't turn to the child next to them. Sometimes children may turn to the next child, but not listen or talk. I have to remind them. Or, I may decide to do a role-play. I will choose a person to represent the child next to me. Then I proceed to ignore her or I talk while she is talking. The children laugh. We discuss what I should be doing. Then we do the role-play again, and we take turns listening and looking, or talking and looking. These small group discussions involve from one to four children. When I am satisfied that children are communicating with each other, I listen in on the conversations so I can get an idea of what the children are thinking about.

THE TEACHER CALLS ON ANYONE DURING A WHOLE CLASS DISCUSSION

Then we have a whole class discussion. I call on several children, whether or not they have raised their hands. Or, I tell a child that I will be calling on her in a few minutes, thereby giving her time to prepare.

THERE IS NO CALLING OUT

You must be called on to speak. Early in the year, we discuss why we have this rule. Perhaps it would be different in a smaller class, but we have at least twenty-six children in our classes. Children must know that everyone must have an opportunity to participate. If children want to get called on, they must raise their hands (although I do call on children who have not raised their hands). Of course, there are children who need reminders about this.

PUT YOUR HANDS DOWN WHEN SOMEONE IS TALKING

No one may raise their hand or talk while another child is talking. The reason is to be fair and to give all children an opportunity to participate. If a child calls out continuously, she may have a time-out or another consequence later. We will have a brief discussion about the issue. She must make a commitment to correct the problem.

THIS IS THE IDEAL

It would be ideal to have a discussion without children raising their hands to be called on. Occasionally there is such enthusiasm that these kinds of discussions do happen. Even during these rare moments, look around to make sure that the same children are not dominating. I usually remind the children to raise hands again. I seldom see the children who tend to dominate voluntarily hold back to let their classmates speak.

LOOK AT THE PERSON WHO'S TALKING

If we are in a circle or a bunch, children are expected to turn to look at the person who is talking. While some children are listening even though they are not looking, others are not listening. Very often, I quietly remind children to look at the person who is talking. Sometimes I give a nonverbal reminder such as looking at a child and directing my hand toward the person who is talking.

LISTEN CAREFULLY

This is a tough one. Both children and adults are so busy formulating their own thoughts about what they will say that they don't hear the person who is talking. Or they are just not listening. Often you'll hear a child say the same thing someone else said just a minute before. We do role-plays where I model listening. I choose a partner. When he is talking, I look the other way. I play with my shoes. I talk. The children laugh. Then we talk about what to do when we're supposed to be listening.

Some teachers promote listening skills by having children tell what their discussion partner or the child before them has said. I do this occasionally.

I find that having children take notes helps their listening skills. Sometimes my students take notes during Research Workshop and Reading Workshop, and they nearly always take notes at interviews.

Compliment good listening. We had a most incredible discussion after I asked, "We've talked about how there used to be no women doctors in the United States. How do you think we got from no women doctors to now, where there are many women doctors? Talk to the people next to you." When we finished the small group discussions and had a whole class discussion, Rina said, "Matthew thought they had to change the law. Donnie thought that they just *let* women become doctors. And I thought they probably had to fight for it." Another child said, "We thought that Martin Luther King must have helped." You could tell that they were listening to each other and were thinking on a high level. You could see the impact of the research they had done earlier in the year when the child referred to Dr. King. (However, the first woman doctor was Elizabeth Blackwell, in the early 1900s way before Dr. King's time.) Of course, they got a huge compliment from me for listening so carefully to each other and for their brilliant thinking.

LAUGH WITH BUT NOT AT OTHERS
We love to laugh in our class, but making fun of someone or their idea or question is totally unacceptable. In the beginning of the year, we discuss why we must not laugh at other people or make fun of what they say or if they fall. Some children need reminders of that all through the year. Children must apologize for laughing at (or making fun of) others. Children who do this repeatedly have a time-out to write an apology.

BE PATIENT
In the beginning of the year, we discuss why we must give certain children extra time to formulate their thoughts. I've had a number of students who process very slowly. It may take them an extra few minutes to prepare to speak in a discussion. No one may talk or raise their hand to speak while we wait. "Hands down while Maria is thinking about her answer." It's a valuable learning experience for children to watch as I help Maria formulate her thoughts. Hopefully they will apply this strategy for helping another child in their lives.

GET FEEDBACK FROM CHILDREN
Often I will ask if there is anyone who does not understand. In the beginning of the year the class discusses why we have to take time to be sure everyone understands. If I see that there are children who don't, we have a discussion, a role-play, or another clarifying activity. I remind the class that we want all children to understand, and those who already understand, must be patient.

GIVE REGULAR FEEDBACK TO THE CHILDREN
I give compliments for different reasons: for great thinking, for speaking up (to someone who is usually quiet), for saying something caring or thoughtful, and so on. These compliments encourage more of that same behavior. Of course, you can also tell children that you are not satisfied with the discussion and explain what you expect.

HAVE CHILDREN GIVE FEEDBACK TO OTHER CHILDREN
Children compliment each other. I love it when children take on this role. Often, I tell them how proud I feel that they are complimenting others (particularly

when children were formerly rather self-centered or selfish). It is empowering for children.

RETHINK YOUR TEACHING

When the discussion is mediocre or not enough children are participating, I quickly ask myself some questions. Is the topic or question worthy of a discussion? Should I pose the question in a different way? Is this the right time for this topic? Perhaps the children have had enough for the moment, and we can save it for another day. The level of discussion is often a reflection of the level of the teaching!

Room Setup

There are lots of books that talk about setting up classrooms. I will talk about some of the things that have been important to me. Classroom setup is strategic. It's based on our goals. The physical classroom must reflect that I want to empower the children, that I want to develop a community, and that our classroom is inquiry-based. While I think about where things should be placed in the classroom, I think also about *preventing problems*. Here are some of the things we have in our room. In some cases, I will talk about how to prevent problems.

TEACHER'S DESK

At MNS teachers don't have the traditional desks at the front of the classroom. This sends a message that the learning is not teacher-centered. Learning is decentralized. It is child-centered. Family members have helped some teachers by building work spaces and storage spaces along a wall, usually near the computers. During the day, I find myself sitting on the carpet or on the rocking chair, sitting or kneeling next to a child who is writing at a table, sitting at a table with a group of children for a formal activity, just walking around the room observing children at work, or meeting informally with groups of children.

OTHER FURNITURE

Isabel Beaton always instructs her student teachers to place shelves and cabinets so you can scan the room from anywhere you are sitting. That means that the shelves and cabinets should not be high. Be sure that furniture doesn't block easy access to the door, the writing center, the coat closet, or supplies.

> *prevention:* Place furniture so that children can move around the room as easily as possible. Sometimes the placement of furniture creates bottlenecks where there are just too many children trying to get to one area. We should try different arrangements to reduce bottlenecks. At times that is not possible.

CUBBIES AND MAILBOXES

Each child has a cubby and a mailbox. This empowers children. They can be independent. It also saves time, as we don't have to wait for monitors to hand things out. The names on the mailboxes are in alphabetical order (except when a child just can't reach the top row of mailboxes or a child is new in the class). Our cubbies are built into the wall of our 100-year-old school.

> *prevention:* Placement of names on the cubbies is strategic. When I know about problem behaviors before the school year begins, I think about that as I assign cubbies. I place cubbies of children who are pokers and pushers or have other such issues far apart so they won't have to interact. I usually give them cubbies at either end so they won't have to interact with as many children when they go to get their journals. When there is a potentially difficult child, I surround her cubby with cubbies of children who are mellow. When there is a child who will need support finding her journals, I place her cubby near those of children who will be helpful to her.

COMPUTER TABLE

This houses a computer and a printer.

OTHER TABLES

We have a hodgepodge of worktables in our room: rectangular, hexagonal, and round. That's what I was able to find around the school when I first started working there. Children can see our word wall, number chart, and alphabet charts from all tables. Children at tables that are further away from the word wall or particular signs on murals or charts, sometimes have to walk closer to them when they are writing to get a better look.

CARPET AT STORY CIRCLE

We have a large, heavy duty carpet at story circle. There is a rocking chair for an adult at one end of the carpet. It's near an easel that holds a dry mark board, markers, and erasers, poems written on large poster board, a dictionary, and a chart tablet. There are several large maps hanging on the wall behind the rocking chair, so that it takes just a moment to point out a location on a map. There are built-in cabinets in the corner next to the rocking chair. They house our poetry and fiction libraries. If they weren't built in, I would have wanted to have some bookshelves which I could reach easily from the rocking chair. We store a vacuum cleaner in the corner of the room so we can clean the carpet regularly.

> *prevention:* The area around the shelf where we have our boxes with writing folders gets congested. I can't think of any other place to put them. So, we have a discussion about it and create a new procedure together: If you see a lot of people getting their folders (writing paper, snacks, etc.), stand back and wait. If necessary, we do a role-play to model this procedure. After several years of such congestion, I finally thought about a new arrangement for the boxes. I spaced the writing boxes out so that there would be lots more space between them.

BULLETIN BOARDS

Placement of displays is strategic. Sit in different parts of your room. Look at the bulletin boards or other places you can display children's work, the word wall, or signs. Think about the prime locations in your room, places that children pass frequently, places that are highly visible. We have two walls with long corkboard bulletin boards.

DRY MARK BOARDS

On a wall, we have a dry mark board for our schedule. We have several small portable dry mark boards the adults use when we work with children in different parts of the room.

WORD WALLS

Our main word wall has high frequency words and is visible from all parts of the room. There are no cabinets or objects that block anyone's view of it. The words are in large print on index cards. Children who can't see the words well from where they are sitting can walk over to the word wall. We have specialty word walls that are related to specific research. One year we had a paleontology word wall that was on the back of a shelf, a health care worker word wall on the doors of a large cabinet, and a child labor and sweatshop word wall on the back of a shelf. Children had to walk over to see those word walls. I reassess my placement and use of the word walls regularly. After having the main word wall in the same place for several years, I decided to move it to improve its visibility.

MURALS

There are some prime locations for murals, and if you want the murals to be noticed more by children, the murals should be placed in these locations. Each room is different. These are the prime locations in our room: near where children line up, near our meeting area, and on the wall we face as we enter the classroom. I designed and our custodian built (with old window poles attached to wall brackets) mural holders in front of the windows so murals could be hung on clips in these prime locations. We have murals in other spots as well, but the ones I want to emphasize are placed in the most visible locations.

WRITING ON SIGNS AND MURALS

Since we encourage the children to use signs and labels to help them spell various words, we want them to have easy access to the words. As much as possible, both children and adults make the print on labels and signs quite large so that it can be seen from a distance. This helps cut down on children needing to walk around. When children are just beginning to write and are using approximated spelling or their writing is not too legible, I use a black marker to rewrite their words below theirs in large, neat print. Later in the year, the children write the words in pencil, we edit, then, they go over the letters with a black permanent marker.

Book Boxes and Shelves

We have bookshelves as well as plastic and cardboard boxes in different parts of the room. Each box is labeled by topic. There are books of different reading levels within each box. The content of the boxes changes depending on the particular research we are doing. Books for our independent reading are on shelves or in boxes and are accessible to children. Special books for guided reading and books we are not using are on shelves which are not accessible to the children.

In the science area there are boxes of books about dogs and cats, the human body, fossils, animals which do jobs, people who work with animals because children are doing nonfiction writing about those topics. In the social studies shelves are boxes of books that relate to our research topics such as vehicles, buildings, and inventions. For our fiction, where we have multiple books by a single author or about a similar topic, we may have a special box.

Paint Area

This small area is a very busy place. There is a board to which we staple butcher paper for painting murals. The floor is covered with paper. There are small containers of paint. Nearly every week children produce one or more murals there.

Block Area

This area is surrounded on three sides by shelves. It's not a large space, but lots of great block building happens there.

Lego Cabinet

There are a few boxes of Legos. A movable cabinet houses the on-going Lego projects.

Placement of Materials

Most of the materials children will be using must be easily accessible to them without getting permission. Some materials are kept in a closet, and children need permission to get them.

Work Supplies

Each table has a supply of regular pencils and erasers, colored pencils, and washable markers supplied by the school and the families. Children have no private school supplies. I send notes home to encourage donations of our shared supplies.

> *prevention:* In my two previous schools the rule was that children had to bring their own sharpened pencils each day and crayons for art class. There was often tension and scolding when children didn't comply. Some teachers refused to let children participate in class activities if they didn't have their own pencil. One teacher even scolded me when I let children borrow our crayons for art class, and she wouldn't let them participate. It is far easier and more pleasant not to have this as

an issue. You save a lot of time, too. When parents send donations of supplies and these are added to any supplies you get from the school supply room, it helps build community.

JOURNALS

Each child has separate journals for reading (purple), math (green), interviews (brown steno pad), and research (blue). I purchase these journals from an office supply store late in the summer when there are big sales. I get reimbursed by the PTA (Parent Teachers Association) or Teacher's Choice (funds from the Board of Education). The journals are kept in the children's cubbies. Children are in charge of their own journals. Of course, if the children buy their own journals, you might suggest a type (hard cover, spiral, steno pad) and let the children select the color.

> *prevention:* Time is of the essence in our classroom. We can't waste time. When everyone has the same color journal or the same color dot for a curriculum area, I can just say, "Bring your purple journal to reading." It's quick and easy. After a while, children know that they should bring their brown journal to an interview. They are in charge of getting their journals.

WRITING FOLDERS

Each child has a colored writing folder. The folders are in five plastic boxes, each with a different color label that matches the colors of the folders. That color coding simply helps children find their folders quickly. This empowers the children.

> *prevention:* When I know before the school year begins that particular children are pokers or pushers or have other such issues, I place their folders in different boxes so they won't have to interact as much. If a child needs extra support, I place her folder in a box with children who are supportive.

Workplaces

There are several different types of seating arrangements for work in our classroom. Having different types of work spaces is especially helpful with a large class. Also, this gives children options. It is empowering for children to make choices about where to sit.

TABLES

We have no assigned seats at the tables. I can see children at the tables from wherever I am sitting, whether that is on a chair or on the carpet.

CARPET AT STORY CIRCLE

We have different seating arrangements at story circle depending on the particular activity.

For individual work Children can grab a clipboard or chalkboard and work anywhere on the carpet during Writing Workshop or while writing a page for a homemade book.

For work with a partner Math partners can choose to work on the carpet when they work with a partner during Math Workshop. Reading partners and children who are writing with a partner can choose to work on the carpet.

For small group work For small group work for reading or Research Workshop, the group working on the carpet usually sits in a circle.

Whole class activities When the whole class is meeting at story circle we have different seating arrangements. The seating assignments are based on several factors:

- Certain children, for academic or behavioral reasons, need to be right up in the front near the teacher. For example, if a child is going through some difficulties at home, you need to be able to have some quiet private conversations and words of support or give a pat on the back.
- Certain children must be separated from others because they distract each other.
- Certain children must be further back because they are constantly bouncing up and down, preventing others from seeing.
- Short children are not required to sit in the front because that isn't fair. I make sure that they sit in between people in the row in front of them or on a chair so they can see. I try to make sure they are not behind children who wiggle too much, so they don't have to keep moving to adjust their view.
- Some children have vision problems or focusing problems, so they should be in the first or second row.
- Some children have trouble sitting on the carpet because of problems with legs, backs, or obesity, so they should be assigned a seat on a chair in the back row or along the side. Others really love to sit on a chair or to be in the back.

Occasionally I move children to a new spot for these reasons:

- A child may request a move.
- A child is sitting next to someone with whom they are fooling around.
- A child needs to sit next to another child who is a better role model.
- A child bounces up and down too much and is preventing others from seeing.
- A child needs to be closer to the dry mark board or the teacher.

For whole class activities at story circle, children sit either in a circle, a semi-circle, or facing the rocking chair. Here are some of our procedures for that:

- *Sitting in a circle*   When children sit in a circle on the carpet, they can easily see the person who is talking. At Math Workshop, they can all see what is happening in the middle of the circle. The children are responsible for moving tables and for moving back so that all children are part of the circle. It's part of being considerate of others. Before the transition to an activity where they will work in a circle, I remind them of this, unless they have that skill down pat already.

    prevention: With a few exceptions, children choose their own spot in the circle. If I must move a child, that move is not permanent. Children can earn the right to choose their own seat again.

- *Sitting in a semi-circle*   This is a relatively new seating arrangement and I'm already very happy with it. Children sit on chairs in a semi-circle along the edges of the carpet. Another group of children sit on the carpet in a semi-circle in front of those chairs. The adult sits in the rocking chair at the other end of the carpet. Children can see each other and the teacher easily. There is a big space in the middle—which is great for role-plays.
- *Sitting in a bunch facing the adult in the rocking chair*   At Meeting Time when we have poetry, singing, and stories, I sit in the rocking chair. At interviews the guest sits in the rocking chair, and I sit on a regular chair right near him. The children sit facing the adult(s). Some children are uncomfortable sitting on the floor and some prefer sitting on chairs, so we usually have a row of chairs in the back.

    prevention: Some years I let children choose where to sit. When I see that it's taking too much time for children to decide where to sit, when children are feeling betrayed by friends who didn't choose to sit next to them, or when there are children with special needs, I assign seats on the carpet. It's a way to prevent problems. There is much less emotional wear and tear for the children, and it takes less time for children to settle down. I have chosen to use the precious time we have for our curriculum work, not the work of sitting down.

Getting in Line

Some children have little trouble lining up while, for others, it's so difficult. They are worried about who their partner will be in line. Why does so and so want to be her partner and not mine? Sometimes there's a lot of anguish. Sometimes making partner choices just takes too long.

prevention: To eliminate this problem, I assign partners or the children select partners—a different person each month. It makes lining up much faster and, for many children, much less painful or complicated.

There is a transition time in the process of getting in line. Children clean up after one activity, then get their coats, book bags, lunch boxes, and so on. Children look for their partner, then they get in line. There will be a lot of movement. That's fine, as long as the movement is directed toward getting in line. Sometimes another adult or I walk over to our very small closet to remind children to get in line. We walk over rather than shout at the children in the closet. It is very important to keep our volume low.

There is a lot of talking at this time. After a few minutes of transition, I give a signal for silence ("Ago"). It seems to cut through the noise. The majority of the children will hear it and will respond. If necessary, I tell the children that this is now a silent time. Again, I remind the stragglers to get in line. I make some announcements. If it's dismissal time, we sing our good-bye song, Woody Guthrie's "So Long, It's Been Good to Know Yuh." Then we say good-bye. As children get familiar with this routine, they do what is expected during the transition.

> *prevention*: Place the children in line strategically. We do not want the children to do the wrong thing and end up in trouble or end up hurting other children. We need to set them up to be good.
>
> I always stand in front of the line (unless a student teacher has taken over). Some children are assigned a special position in the line. They must stay in that position every day. I place children in the front if they have behavior problems—the hitters, the pokers, the "fool arounders." You (or another adult) need to be able to see the children whose behavior may present a problem. If they are near the end of the line, you can't see them as your class goes around the bend in a stairway. They can earn the right to move further back in the line as their behavior improves. You have to check each time before the class goes anywhere that these particular children are in the correct place in line. Keeping an eye on this group of children can prevent trouble. That's what we want to do—prevent problems.
>
> Sometimes I walk with a child who has a disability, such as inability to navigate the steps, or a child who otherwise needs the supervision of an adult. If there is another adult to assist, the child can stand further back in the line. We want to prevent that child from getting hurt.

There are some children who have real difficulty following the steps in this routine. They will need support. However, when a child simply disregards the routine, I tell him in a serious voice to get in line. The next day, I will quietly remind him of my expectations. When children show disrespect for the guidelines about the line, there are consequences.

Preparing for Lunch and Recess

Children have less supervision at lunch and recess than in our classrooms. Kids who have behavior problems in the classroom often get in trouble, get hurt, get their feelings hurt, and so much more at lunch and recess. What can we do?

Before lunch, when the children are in line, I give a signal for silence. I use a low, serious voice to review the rules for lunch. It's not a discussion. Or I may ask different children to state the rules for lunch. (Stay at the table unless you are throwing things away. Get permission from an adult to use the bathroom.) Some are school rules and others were created by the class. There is no need to have a prolonged discussion of the reasons for these rules. They just need to be restated by me or the children. Then I say, "I expect you to follow these rules when you are at lunch and recess today. I want to be very proud of you when I speak to the teachers at lunch about your behavior." After a while, we review lunch rules only when I see that some children are a bit jumpy or have had problems with self-control during the morning.

> *prevention:* There are days when you can predict there will be problems at lunch time: before long weekends or major holidays, certain kinds of weather conditions, days when your schedule has been changed, days when the children seem particularly jumpy, and so on. On those days, it is very important to use a serious tone and remind the children of the lunchtime rules and your expectations. I will usually end this short speech with something like this: "I expect excellent behavior."

Dealing with Lunch and Recess

Most schools struggle with lunch- and recess-time. Each school system has different contractual agreements. In New York City, teachers no longer have to do lunch duty, so school aides watch the children. The administration is ultimately in charge.

- Our school has lunch clubs such as chess, dance, art, jazz, and so on. Families pay for these clubs. Some scholarships are available. Besides having wholesome activities, it reduces the number of children in the school yard.
- Our school has secured permission from the police department to close the street in front of the school at recess and lunchtime. Our fourth and fifth graders have recess in the street. The younger children play in the small school yards. We have kindergarteners and first graders in the same lunch period as fourth graders. We have two lunch sessions.
- Our school recently purchased large, round folding tables. These seem to be more conducive to conversation, card games, and other activities than our former, long, rectangular tables.

- Children are supposed to remain at their seats except to throw things away or use the bathrooms. That limits the traffic.
- Sometimes sharing of meals and desserts becomes a problem. There are children who impose on others, who demand that others give them food, and so on. Since I'm not there to help negotiate that, I may impose a no-sharing-food rule or children may decide together to have that rule.
- Family members are encouraged to volunteer during recess and lunch. This is invaluable. There may be some family members who are not as helpful as they might be. Some come to feed their own child and don't help out the class. To avoid this, it's important to have a meeting early in the year or periodically during the year to talk about how volunteers can best participate. Or, you may want to stop by the lunchroom, observe, and find time to meet with a particular adult.

It's important for schools to make this time as safe and as peaceful as possible. Some schools have committees or even faculty discussions about this issue.

Dealing with Recess on Snowy or Rainy Days

In a previous school where I taught, 300 children sat in the auditorium on a rainy day. They watched a video that was difficult to hear because of the talking by children and the shouting over the bullhorns by adults. It was a totally inhumane and unacceptable situation that only provoked inappropriate behavior. At MNS we have a few different options for these days. Teachers may choose from these options.

- Some teachers choose to have their classes go to the auditorium (from which all seats have been removed). Children can watch a video, read, draw, or use the games that are available. They are supervised by school aides.
- Some classes join together in one classroom where they can draw or play with what we call rainy or snowy day boxes. These are shoebox-size plastic boxes the families have filled with small toys, games, or art materials. Another first grade class comes to our room where my children shared their rainy day boxes. They are supervised by school aides. I always choose this option because I find it the most peaceful for my students. There may be fifty-five children in the room, but, after a few reminders in the beginning of the year, it's usually rather quiet and calm.
- Some children go to lunch clubs.

Calming Down After Lunch and Recess

Lunch and recess can be traumatic. When I get the children in line after lunch, we head to the stairway. I let the children talk during this time. Once we go up the stairs, my class must be silent. It's a school rule that is enforced unevenly. I have chosen to enforce it. It makes life so much easier and much calmer. I raise my hand and give the V or the peace sign to remind the children there must be silence. I may say, "Excuse me," and remind the one or two children to be quiet. I calmly say "*Ago*" only if children continue talking. After a while, most children in my class calm down and walk quietly without adult intervention.

Here are some things we do:

PRIVATE CONVERSATIONS

While I minimize discussion about lunchtime problems, some must be addressed. If the problem involved only one or two children, I may bring those children to the front of the line with me, and we will talk quietly about the problem as we go up to the room. Or, I might tell the few children that I will meet with them at Center Time to resolve the problem.

CLASS DISCUSSIONS

If there were lunch and recess problems that involved many children, we may have a whole class discussion at story circle when we get back to the room. We talk about the problem and then do some problem solving. We think together about how children could have acted differently, and what we will do to solve that kind of problem in the future. When children are part of that process, you empower them to find solutions to their own problem situations.

MEETING

Most days, children simply put their coats and lunch boxes away and walk over to story circle for Meeting. The children know that this will be a pleasant and calm time. It will be a relief from all the noise and clatter of lunch and recess. It soothes the soul. This is our ritual. We say "Good afternoon" to each other. Then we recite familiar poems and/or learn a new one. I play my guitar, and we sing some familiar songs and/or learn a new song. Last year one of the mothers, Lisa Rizzi, sang with us every Tuesday afternoon. Then we have a read aloud and a discussion. The length of time for each of those activities depends on other demands of our schedule. Often, it's a joyous time.

The Bathroom

Hopefully your school doesn't require you to take all of your children to the bathroom at the same time. They had that policy at one school where I worked. It was a grand waste of time. At MNS children are sent to the bathrooms alone or with a partner. The bathrooms for younger children are unisex. It would make sense to always send children to the bathroom when they ask to go. However, there are children who use this as an opportunity to take a break, to play, or to get into mischief. You must use your judgment when deciding whether or not to let these children go and hope with all your heart that you do not make a mistake. Most teachers have had the horrible experience of telling a child to wait and then seeing the urine trickling down the child's leg.

This is what I do about bathroom use:

- I tell the children that the best times for using the bathroom are during transitions, snack time, lunch and recess time, and Center Time. I discourage use of the bathroom during work time, except when absolutely necessary.
- I tell the children that they should go to the bathroom, wash their hands, and return quickly and quietly to the classroom. There needs to be consequences if someone stays way too long in the bathroom to play. But don't always assume that the child was playing—sometimes there is a line, and some children take a while to go to the bathroom. If I am certain that a child was fooling around and didn't get to do his work, he must do the work at Center Time. He will have time-out from Center Time or even have to write a note home for more serious things such as standing on toilet seats, throwing wads of toilet paper, vandalizing the bathroom, and so on.
- Children have to ask an adult before they go to the bathroom. Some children very cleverly ask the student teachers instead of me because they assume the student teacher will just say yes. When a child abuses bathroom privileges, he has to ask me personally.

prevention: When I see certain patterns in bathroom use by a child, I think about ways to change that. For example, Ronnie always asked to go to the bathroom during Writing Workshop. He stayed out for at least ten minutes, wandered back to his seat, and hardly got engaged in the writing. I pointed out that pattern to Ronnie. We talked about his discomfort with writing. He really struggled with getting started with the writing. The bathroom was a way to avoid writing. We discussed ways to work on the writing issue. We had an agreement that he could go to the bathroom during Writing Workshop for an emergency only. He would ask to go, and I would say, "Is it an emergency?" If he said it was, I would say, "Hurry back" or "Be back before I count to twenty." Ronnie knew that I didn't mean that literally. But he would hurry back because he knew I would be looking for him to return.

Cleanup

In our class, cleanup is part of every activity. It is everyone's responsibility. Our goal is to have children see cleanup as a natural part of each activity and to have them be conscious of their responsibility to the class. Of course, some children already have that sense of responsibility, and others have lots of work to do in that area. After a while, with a few exceptions, the cleanup is directed by the children. They are empowered to make the room a pleasant place to be. Little by little, children internalize that responsibility.

Job charts? For many years I posted job charts in the room. Children changed jobs weekly. I was never comfortable with those charts because they took up so much time, so I decided to abandon them. It's always a good idea to reassess your routines.

Some teachers have job charts for special kinds of jobs such as watering the plants, feeding the various pets, being a monitor, marking the day on the calendar, and so on. While I don't have such charts, I think they can be useful.

Here's what we do:

- Before the end of all activities (Writing Workshop, Research Workshop, Center Time, etc.) I remind the children about putting their things away and cleaning the area around them. They know that means that when they finish their area, they can straighten up other parts of the room.

  For example, at the end of Writing Workshop, I say, "Put your folders away and be sure to clean up." If some children just put their folders away and start talking or go to get their jackets for recess, I will interrupt the cleanup and say, "*Ago,*" the children respond "*Ame,*" and I compliment the children who are cleaning up areas. I am especially quick to compliment children who are cleaning up beyond the area where they worked. "I love the way Noah put the wallpaper samples away, and he didn't even have his book covered today. That's great, Noah." Other times I sing the compliments.

- When Center Time is ending, I remind the class that it's time to stop their activities and to clean up. They know that means you clean the area where you were working or playing. When you are done, you:

  clean the common areas—the tables and the floor.

  help people who haven't finished cleaning—the blocks, the tables that are slimy from the snails, and so on

  put the chairs in piles of five so the custodian can clean the floor.

- The whole class works until the room is clean. The children come to know that this is expected. During the whole process, I scan the room to see if everyone is helping. I may tell children who are fooling around or who are not engaged to do a specific job. Visitors are surprised to see how well the children clean up with so little adult involvement. Toward the end of that cleanup, I indicate to the children that they can get their coats and book bags when they are finished.

Part 2: Problems

Some people say, "Teachers have it easy. They work until three and have summers off." I love teaching and get great joy from it, but teaching is not easy. This section addresses the times when teaching can be especially difficult.

Solving Problems

We have procedures for when children have difficulties working or playing with others. So often, children don't see the adults at home using good strategies to solve problems. Many children see their parents screaming. Some are exposed to violence. Some see one parent remain passive and not even attempt to solve problems. School is an important place to work on problem solving.

CHILDREN SOLVING PROBLEMS ON THEIR OWN

The optimum solution is to have children solve problems without an adult. For some, this takes lots of practice. Sometimes we even do role-plays to demonstrate problem solving skills such as speaking in a calm voice, listening, and coming up with solutions that work for both people. I may ask children to sit together at a table or step outside the room to discuss what happened and how they can resolve the problem. They just have to let me know how they chose to resolve it. This approach empowers children. I compliment children when they problem solve without an adult.

THE TEACHER TALKING WITH A SMALL NUMBER OF CHILDREN

If just one or two children are involved, we may go to the side and talk. (If we can't take time to talk about it at that moment, I tell the children that we will talk later or during Center Time.) We try to clarify what happened. I ask each child what happened. I may ask whether what they did was appropriate or inappropriate. I ask why the child did what they did. Children may not interrupt each other. I usually work with the children to help them think of ways to resolve the problem. I may ask the children to step aside or go to the hall to continue talking without any adult intervention. Or, if they can't find a way to get started with the discussion, I may tell them how I want them to solve the problem. Perhaps I will send one or both children to another area to work or play (at Center Time). There may be apologies, if necessary. I may give either or both children a time-out or another consequence for their inappropriate behavior.

It's very important that, if there is a consequence, the children restate what they did that was inappropriate and what they plan to do the next time. Here is a typical exchange.

Teacher: Do you know why you are having a time-out?
Child: I hit Joey.

Teacher: Was that appropriate or inappropriate?
Child: Inappropriate.
Teacher: What will you do next time Joey bothers you?
Child: I won't hit him.
Teacher: What else could you do?

The children could offer several other solutions such as: "Ask him to stop bothering you," "Try to make friends," or "Speak to an adult." Of course, there are many variations.

THE WHOLE CLASS WORKING TOGETHER TO SOLVE PROBLEMS

When problems involve many children, we take time to have a whole class discussion. Or if it involves a few children but I think we need the help of the class, we have a whole class discussion. This is our usual process:

1. state the problem(s)
2. make mention that it wasn't everyone (if there were children who were not involved)
3. briefly try to find reasons for that inappropriate behavior
4. collectively find solutions. We may do role-plays of the possible solutions.
5. We may, instead, begin the process by reading a relevant story (see Chaper 8).

I don't really like the whole class getting involved in determining consequences for a specific child or children. It seems too much like a court. However, the class may discuss proposals for what should happen in the future. Here is a typical exchange: I begin with a serious tone, a low voice. I say, "I was shocked to get that report from _____ (a school aide) that there were so many children who were running around the lunchroom. I know that some of you were in your seats, and I compliment you for that." I may ask why children chose to run around. Then I say, "I do not want this to happen again. What are we going to do to solve this problem?" We will get several suggestions. We don't vote on the best or most popular solution. I choose one or more of the solutions that I think is appropriate. I then ask what the consequence should be in the future if people break the rules we have agreed upon. However, I make the final decision. The next day before lunch, I will remind the class of our lunchroom procedures.

GIVE POSITIVE FEEDBACK

When a child makes an effort and works at problem solving, I compliment him. I might say, "I am so proud of the way Tony plays in the block area. He's not hitting any more. How wonderful! Wow, that's great. I'm going to tell your parents,

Tony." Or, "Kim is like a new child—no more calling out, no more meanness. Ahhh, this is a great day. I am so proud of you Kim. I can't wait to tell your mother about this. Wow!" Of course, for older children, you will give the compliment but choose different words.

Often, other children will also compliment the child. That way, the whole class takes responsibility for improving behavior. (Use your judgment about whether you want the whole class involved in certain situations.)

Working with a Child Who Won't Listen

Remember that in the beginning of the year children are *approximating* appropriate behavior. There will be repeat problems. Some children seem to find it necessary to "test the system" to see if you really mean it. Some do not have structures in place at home and don't respond right away to classroom structures. Some think that rules don't apply to them. Some children have already formed a pattern of misbehavior. Some have seen terrible examples at home and are merely imitating that. If you are consistent with your enforcement, gradually children will let up from the testing and will behave appropriately. It usually happens that way. Then teaching becomes easier.

Some parents and teachers "over discuss" problems. You can find yourselves talking so much, there are no behavior changes, and so much time is wasted. You can't always stop and discuss every repeat infraction. Use your judgment. You may decide to skip the discussion, tell the child (or children) that his behavior was inappropriate, and give the consequence.

INVOLVING FAMILIES

I prefer to resolve problems within the classroom. When a child is unable or unwilling to change inappropriate behavior, I have the child write a note home stating the problem, or I talk with the family on the phone, write a note, or talk in person. I state the problem. We talk about possible reasons for the problem. Often, there is a similar problem at home, so I ask about that. Sometimes there is not. Or sometimes a family member will deny that there is a problem at home. When you get to know a family better, they may open up and tell you more.

I tell the family member about what we have done to try to solve the problem in school. We talk about how we can work together to resolve the problem. We try to establish the same rules for school and home, so the child knows we are working together. We talk about consequences at home and at school. We schedule a time to talk about the problem again: after school, in a week, in two weeks, and so on. Sometimes we agree that I will send a note home, talk to the parent in the school yard, or call every day until we see a change. I make a big deal about it when there is a positive change. I let the family know how happy I am about this. Family members do love to hear good news.

Sometimes a child or family member doesn't want to hear that their child had a time-out or other consequence and gets very angry. Perhaps they thought their child could do no wrong or just that the punishment was not appropriate for their child. Sometimes we are wrong. It's a good idea to think about what the family member said. Maybe we think we are right, and we simply disagree with the family.

Consequences at home should meet the infraction Over the years I've heard parents punish their children in so many ways. One mother said, "Oh, you're not going to Tia's house in the Dominican Republic this summer!" I told her that won't work because you know you plan to send your child there while you're at work. One mother told her child she would be sent to foster care if she didn't improve. Her brother was already in foster care. One parent threatened that Santa wouldn't bring any presents. Another parent threatened to leave her child in Mexico if she didn't do her homework. The child broke down weeping to me because she really did believe the threat but she wasn't quite sure. Sometimes that idle threat is terrifying to a child. When a child realizes it's an idle threat, the threat is ineffective. Some of these threats are really quite mean and may have a negative impact on a child.

So often parents lack strategies for disciplining their children. They may do what their parents did to them. They jump right over any nonviolent solutions, and resort to hitting or whipping their children. There have been many times when I feared telling families about a child's inappropriate behavior for fear they would beat the child. Tragically, one mother beat her child so badly after he bit a classmate at lunchtime, the child was taken from her by the child welfare department. Sometimes I have reminded families that in this country, it's against the law to beat your child (I'm not talking about a simple spanking).

Out of frustration or lack of strategies, parents sometimes threaten or even carry out consequences that are too big for the situation. Taking time to discuss nonviolent options with families is really important. Sometimes I'll ask a parent what the child really loves to do at home: TV, gameboy, videogames, computer games, Nintendo, play with certain toys, and so on. I'll suggest taking one of those away until there is an improvement in behavior. Other possibilities include sitting on a chair for a while, not getting a certain toy the child had hoped for, not going to the movies. We also talk about doing positive things with your child: going for walks; spending special time with one parent; going to a museum, zoo, or library; and so on. These talks with families can make a big difference in the quality of parenting and the quality of the child's home life. An improvement at home always makes a big difference in school.

Rewards?

Generally, I'm not an advocate for points or rewards for things children are expected to do. Some children come to expect rewards. I think we must work to help them internalize and follow the rules and guidelines at home and at school. (Of course, most of us have tested many a rule in our lifetimes!) I prefer to compliment a child:

- just to the child
- in front of the class
- directly to the family
- to colleagues and administrators
- and even in front of guests

In addition to compliments, appropriate behavior brings restoration of rights: selecting one's own partner for the line or other activities, sitting in different places at story circle, choosing which research group to be in, and so on. This empowers the child, but it's empowerment with responsibility.

In some difficult situations, I have found that a reward was useful in changing behavior. For some children, we quietly set a goal. For example, I may say, "Laura, if I see that you can _____ for two whole weeks, I will be so proud of you, I'm going to take you to lunch at the pizza shop." That lunch together can make all the difference in the world. Of course, you must get permission from the family.

When changing behavior is a real struggle for a child, I may decide to put a homemade star on a paper or dry mark board every time I see the child doing the right thing. Often the class will spontaneously clap when the child gets several stars. (Of course, it's a relief to them when the child is doing the right thing.) They know I am proud when they compliment other children. I use this strategy only when absolutely necessary.

Involving Colleagues

I send children to colleagues to show them their work so they can get positive feedback. Sometimes I send them with a note about improved behavior. Sometimes teachers in our school send children to each other's rooms for a time-out. That can break the tension in a difficult situation. It's good to talk with colleagues about how to solve a problem with a particular child.

Involving the Administration

I prefer to send a child to the principal to show her his beautiful or improved work or behavior. If I do involve the administration in dealing with behavior problems, I rarely send the child to the principal. Usually, I will talk to the administrator alone or with the family. Sometimes, we choose to have the child present at the meeting so the child can see that the adults are working together to resolve the problem.

Working with a Child You Don't Particularly Like

Let's be honest. It can happen. I have a rule for myself about that. I tell myself and student teachers, "Don't hate a child. Don't dislike a child. If you do, you cannot be an effective teacher." So, what if you do feel that way? Here are some suggestions.

- Step back and do a lot of thinking.
- Ask yourself questions: Why do I feel this way? If it's just the child I don't like, why? Does the child have a mean streak? Is the child arrogant? Is the child giving me a really hard time? Is it me, or is it the child? Do my feelings reflect the way I feel about the child's parents?
- If my feelings reflect the way I feel about the child's parents, I follow this rule: Don't take out feelings about parents on the child. It's not the child's fault. Do everything in your power to separate your feelings about the child and the family. Yes, there are families that are mean, arrogant, neglectful, dysfunctional, and so on. Our job as educators is to do the best possible for the child. While it's great to be able to influence families, it's not always possible. However, we must be there for the child. That's our responsibility. Under these circumstances, we should be very careful not to antagonize the parents, so we don't make it more difficult to work with the child. I've had situations where I just didn't discuss the child's behavior with the family because earlier attempts resulted in the child getting beaten at home or parents going "out of control." It's better in such situations to deal with the problems in school and either minimize talk with the family or talk about anything positive you can possibly think of regarding the child.
- If my negative feelings just reflect how I feel about the child, my rule for myself is to consider this child a special challenge. I think about what I can do in one year to turn that behavior around. I think about what I might have to do to change my own behavior so that I can be more effective. I think about how I can involve the family, the classmates, or other staff to turn the child's behavior around. I don't want to send the child to the next grade without seriously attempting to change that behavior.

Here is an example. I had a student we'll call Andrew. Often he was just not nice. I tried the usual things to turn his behavior around: I talked with him and told him what I expected of him, I made him apologize when he offended others, and I gave him time-out when he offended others. I talked with his parents and with my colleagues. Nothing worked.

That's when I started losing sleep thinking about Andrew. I racked my brains to find a strategy that would work. Looking back, I can see two major strategies that worked:

1. *Curriculum.*   Andrew loved our research. For several months that year we focused our People at Work research on child labor and sweatshops. Andrew got very involved. His parents were also enthusiastic and sent in resources for our research. I noticed that Andrew was empathetic about others. He really cared and was concerned about people who were working under such terrible conditions. Knowing that he cared, even if it was about people who were far away, was very important. He did have feelings. He did have compassion. It was step one. Developing that empathy for people in the immediate world around him, his classmates and others, was the next step.

2. *Involving Andrew in correcting his own behavior.*   During Writing Workshop one day, when the children were all at work, I kneeled down next to Andrew and talked quietly to him. I told him about my thinking and my concerns about his behavior. I told him about my plan to help him become a better person. I gave him several examples of things that other children in our class had done that I considered "sweet." This included children who helped each other, children who supported each other, children who were able to compliment others, and so on. I told Andrew that I wanted people to think of him as "sweet."

Now, that might sound really corny to you, and it was corny, but, it worked! (I would not have used the word *sweet* with an older child.) I told Andrew that I wanted him to be in charge of his own behavior, and that every time I thought he was being a good person, I would be so proud of him.

Over the next several weeks, I praised Andrew constantly, every time he did even the slightest thing that was "sweet." I had spoken to his previous teacher and the principal about this plan, so when I sent Andrew to each of them with a note about his wonderful behavior, they complimented him. I told his parents about the plan and told them about all of the compliments and the positive developments.

Yes, there was a change. Andrew did make changes in his attitude and behavior. His compassion on a global level deepened. I grew to really like Andrew. In third grade he asked his friends to give him money to help start a school in the mountains of Ecuador rather than to give him birthday presents. He wrote to me about that, knowing that I would be really pleased. And I was. My students then sent hundreds of dollars of school supplies for the school.

Working When You're Tired

It's not the children's fault that you're tired. They should not get the brunt of your exhaustion. There have been many times when I went to bed too late, didn't sleep well, or when I had just too many evening events (meetings, activities related to my children, company, and so on). Not even the cup of coffee helped much. Children can read us very well. In the past I found that I had less patience when I was tired. When we are low energy, some children seem to step right in to test our patience or aggravate us. Here are some solutions:

WORK ON YOUR MENTAL ATTITUDE

Try to rise above your exhaustion. Tell yourself, "I'm going to have a good day. I will not take this out on the children. We must have a good day." Children can read us so well, so we should make every effort not to give in to our exhaustion. We should not lower our standards for our teaching or our behavior.

CREATE ENERGY-PRODUCING ACTIVITIES AND EVENTS

Donald Graves once interviewed me and a number of other teachers about what gives us energy to teach. He asked us to take notes for an entire week, noting things in our day that gave us energy, took away energy, or wasted energy. It's a good thing to do. Then, on a day when you are particularly tired or need energy, try to create situations where those positive behaviors can emerge.

ADJUST THE CURRICULUM

On days when I'm particularly tired, I adjust the curriculum. I may make it more ambitious, more hands-on, more active for the children. For example, I was totally exhausted one morning and my student teacher who was leading the paleontology research group would not be in that day. Before school, I thought of a paleontology activity for the whole class. The activity would answer one of their questions about fossils, but it was certainly not what I had originally planned. I needed something that would be fun and energizing for me. So, I sat there before school and laid out a rubber mat and newspapers. On a large tray, I buried bones and real fossils in sand that I mixed with soil. I broke off some small branches from a flower display to make pretend trees, then used some blocks from our block area to prop up the tray so it formed a hill.

When the children came in and saw all of this plunked in the middle of the room, they were excited. That gave me energy. We had a ball, creating storms and pouring water down the slope. Every once in a while, plastic dinosaur bones, chicken bones, and real fossils were exposed by the erosion. A large basin absorbed the water from the storms. Periodically I selected children who mopped up the overflow with sponges. We laughed and shouted with glee, all the way through a marvelous lesson about erosion. What a great way to find out how bones were exposed to paleontologists after millions of years. The activity lasted way too long, but it was a good one. It helped me gather the energy for the rest of that really fine day.

CHOOSE A DIFFERENT BOOK TO READ

If you're going to read a book, select one you're sure the children will like. This will lift the energy for the book talk after you read.

LOOK FOR SOMETHING SPECIAL TO RAVE ABOUT

At Writing Workshop, really search for a gem hidden in someone's writing, especially a child who's not known for his writing. Stop the workshop to read the child's work. Show your delight by your expression, or the enthusiasm in your voice. Ask for comments from other children. Lifting one child can in turn lift you.

TRY TO LAUGH

Children love laughter. It energizes everyone.

AVOID "FILLER" ACTIVITIES

Having children color, copy, or do potentially boring or "filler" activities (busy work) is not a good solution. Boring activities are just that—boring. When met with boring or meaningless work, some children act out. Who can blame them?

TRY ANOTHER APPROACH

On some occasions over the years I have told the children that I am very tired. Just recently I had gotten up periodically through the night to watch the meteorite shower—which I never did get to see because of the proximity of my house to the lights of New York City. I told the children why I was so tired. I told them that when I am tired, I try even harder to be a good teacher, as a way of setting an example for them. Of course, it isn't necessary to explain why you are tired. On a few occasions, I have I told my students why I was tired, just because I think it is important for them to see their teacher as a real human being. For example, when my sons were young, I remember telling the children that I was tired because my son was sick during the night, and I was up with him. There have even been a few times when I have told the children that I am very tired and have asked them to make every effort to have excellent behavior.

Working When You're Upset

Everyone has rough times in their lives. We have to work through the death of loved ones, illness, divorce, disappointments, and so much more. In Chapter 3 I wrote about working during a divorce. Your mental attitude about teaching is critical in these situations. During these times, it helps if you can view your teaching as a diversion from your troubles. Teaching has been my salvation during the most difficult times of my life.

If you have already established a schedule, rituals, and routines, that will be a great source of comfort and organization. Keep to that schedule so that the flow of the day will feel the same for you and the children. On difficult days, I say to myself that I am going to do the best teaching possible. I close the door and try to leave my personal problems outside. I force my mind to focus on the children. I remind myself that it is not the children's fault that I am having a problem, so do not impose my problem on them. I follow a plan similar to the plan for when I am exhausted.

The supreme test of this theory came in April 2003 when my mother was diagnosed with a fast-growing brain tumor. In this situation I actually had to be absent quite often to be with my mother in Buffalo.

We arranged to have the same substitute most of the days I was absent during my mother's illness. That was important for the stability of the children. The children knew the schedule, and the routines and rituals well, so the substitute didn't have to deal with that.

We had already had such a wonderful school year. These were my first absences. Family members pitched in to help in the classroom. The families were absolutely patient, understanding, and supportive. My mother died on July 7, 2003. When I returned to my classroom between my visits to my parents' home in Buffalo, remaining focused was painfully difficult. How I forced myself to heed my own advice.

Dealing with Monday Mornings or the Day After Vacations

How easy is it for you to snap into gear on Monday mornings, particularly after a three-day weekend or a holiday? That's a tough time for many adults. For the children, many have been up later at night. Some have been out and about. Some have spent time with babysitters or with a noncustodial parent. For whatever reasons, children often walk in on Monday morning and are tired, daydreamy, or disconnected. Here are some suggestions for dealing with this:

- Do everything in your power to lift your own emotions. Rise above the children. Use your energy to lift the children out of that Monday morning stupor. Sometimes we even have to have our students stand and stretch or jump up and down. I put energy into my voice and enthusiasm into the teaching. We laugh.
- Some children will need a quick, quiet, private talk. You or another adult can help them process their emotions, and then encourage them to participate in the class activities.
- Some children need some time to adjust and need to be left alone for a short time. They can sit with the other children, but just don't push them to participate right away.
- Children who have been with a noncustodial parent often need time to process what they have experienced. That's not to say that the experience was negative, but usually the two households are run differently, and children need time to move emotionally from one home to another. Use your

judgment about whether to have a quiet talk or to leave them alone when they first arrive in class.

Dealing with Children Before Holidays or Vacations

Of course, children get very excited before three-day weekends or major vacations. This is a tough time. The weeks before the bigger holidays or vacations can be very difficult. The time before Christmas and Chanukah is especially trying. The children are anticipating presents, trips, guests at home, and so on. The hype on the radio and TV gets worse by the day, setting up huge expectations. Some may have exaggerated notions of what presents they will receive. Homes are usually quite busy with shopping, baking, incoming relatives, and so on. Some children love the holidays and others dread them. Many breakups of families occur during these stressful holiday times. People with mental health problems often find holidays particularly difficult. Some families who travel for the holiday choose to leave a few days early or return a few days late. These children are excited about vacation even earlier, and they miss the classroom activities and experiences. It's a complicated situation.

The children are often excited and unfocused in class. Chaos is not fun for you or for the children—*so you need to act quickly to prevent it.* Teaching at this time is not easy, but there are lots of things you can do to make this time workable.

- Remind yourself that both you and the children are excited about the upcoming vacation, and that is normal. Please don't be angry with the children.
- When you first feel that preholiday excitement in the air—the wiggly, bouncy, loud, and/or distracted children, it's time for *the talk.* Ignore the schedule so carefully written on the board. Give a signal for silence. Tell everyone to sit down at a meeting area without books, pencils or any other distractions. Remember, body language is important. Look solemn. Look serious. Keep your voice very low. *No shouting. No meanness.* Tell the children that you know they are excited about the upcoming holiday. Tell them that you are, too. Remind them that we have work to do. Tell them your expectations: pay attention (or, as I say, stay focused on your work), remain silent in the stairway and hallways where others are working, follow the same rules we always have for our class, and so on. Of course, the rules for each class are different.

  When you keep that low, serious tone in your voice, it usually settles the class down for the day. You must be strict. You may have do stop work at other times during the day to remind the children of your expectations. Before lunch or recess you should probably do the same thing. You need to be quick to deal with violations of the rule, just to have the children see that you are absolutely serious.

- Stick to your basic schedule and routines as much as possible. This is particularly important if your school has planned concerts, special assemblies, and other events. Many children are thrown off balance by major changes in the schedule. After a special schoolwide event, give your class a chance to sit calmly and perhaps talk about that event. Tell them you realize that this has been a jumbled day, but you're proud that they have handled it so well. Acknowledge that the mixed-up schedule is difficult for you, too.

    Acknowledge that it is a special time of year. That doesn't mean that you have to have holiday-related activities. But, you may decide that this is a special time to do activities around the issue of peace or helping others. You might choose to write special poetry, paint or draw a peace mural, learn or sing songs about peace, write your own songs, hear stories, write letters to the President, make peace mobiles, and so on. You might collect food for a soup kitchen or clothing and toys for a homeless shelter. Some of these special activities can become part of Writing Workshop or Math Workshop (sorting and organizing clothes and toys or counting cans).
- Make a few changes that will enable the children who are so excited, anxious, and/or unfocused to let go a little. For example, if the children work really hard and well that day, give them a longer Center Time. You may want to add a few special activities—perhaps an art activity.
- Plan well. Be sure that there are hands-on activities built into the plan. Sloppy planning at this time is certain to spell problems.

Dealing with Tired Children

Most of us have had students who have fallen asleep in class or children who are too exhausted to work. Some children really misbehave when they are tired. Here are some suggestions for dealing with this:

- Let a child take a rest and put his head down on the table.
- Have a child work near you so you can help her with self-control.
- Have a quiet talk with the child. Tell him that you know he is tired and remind him of your expectations.
- Compliment a child who you know is very tired but is working at participating or at having self-control.
- Speak to the school nurse. Sometimes the exhaustion is the result of a medical or mental health problem. (I had a child who didn't wake up after a

long bus ride home from the Bronx Zoo. Her body was limp. It turned out that she had anemia, but her parents hadn't been giving her the medication, and they hadn't told me about their child's condition. We encouraged the parents to give the child her treatments.)

- Write a reminder in the weekly homework about early bedtimes. I recommend 8:00 P.M. for first grade. Parents tell me they love that because they can tell their child, "Paula said 8:00."
- Write a note home or call.
- Have a meeting with the family to find ways to resolve the problem. Sometimes when there are parents who work in the evening, when there are babysitters, when there are older siblings, when it is an adult-centered household, when a child has difficulty sleeping, it's really hard to make a change. It doesn't hurt to try.

Dealing with Administrators

Try to work cooperatively with administrators. That's not always easy. In my thirty-one years of teaching at three schools, I've worked with the best and the some who were mediocre. I've been with brilliant educators and wonderful human beings. I've been with the screamers and shouters, the parent-haters, administrators who prided themselves on making children cry, and worse. The best advice is to be the very best teacher you can be:

- Do a really good job teaching reading, writing, and math.
- Strive to develop a rich curriculum in social studies and/or science.
- Work hard on classroom management skills.
- Work closely with the families.
- Be on time in the morning.
- Keep your personal absences to a minimum.
- Give administrators as little to complain about as possible.
- Pick your battles. If you are a new teacher, be very careful. If you do want to do things out of the norm, pick your battles. You may have to make some compromises. If something is particularly important to you and your students, then stand up for it.
- Think carefully before you go to have a talk about a burning issue with the administrator. Try to be calm and collected before you go to talk. Do not go in crying. Many years ago, an administrator made me change classrooms the day before school began. I had worked for weeks during the summer to set up my classroom. It was beautiful and ready for the children to come in and get right to work. I discussed the situation with the principal. When

he was unyielding, I burst into tears, something I regret to this day. I did have to pack and move tons of boxes. For some administrators, being in a position of power over the teachers is very important, sometimes more important than the needs of the children, the faculty, or the families. All you can do in that kind of situation is keep reminding yourself that you are there for the children, do the best you can, and do your crying when you are with colleagues with whom you are close or with friends and family.

If you follow these guidelines, then, when you do something off the beaten path that may upset the administrator, you can point to how well your students are reading or writing. In one school where I taught, the principal did not like family involvement. However, the principal knew that I was doing a good job teaching the academic skills; in fact, family members often went to her to say that. I introduced a peace curriculum and other social studies curriculum that were not part of the Board of Education plan. That principal left me alone to do that curriculum. Family members learned to avoid passing by the principal on the way to our room, so there were only a few problems with family involvement.

Ending the School Year Gracefully

I love to teach, but June is not my favorite time of year. Children begin thinking about summer vacations, the weather gets very hot, some children become restless, and some worry about leaving the teacher or classmates. I don't like the feeling of building a community over the course of a year and then losing that community in June. But, it's our responsibility to bring closure to the year and to make those last few weeks as pleasant as possible for ourselves and the children. Here are some suggestions:

- Do not stop teaching. Do not give children busy work to pass the time. Keep planning. You may want to change the nature of the plans but make every effort to keep most of the regular routines and schedule.
- Plan culminating events as close to the end of the year as possible. This way you can keep building. For example, we have a Family Celebration in the evening, usually mid-June. We usually present songs and plays. We have a birthday party for the children with summer birthdays the last week of school. Other teachers have poetry readings or book readings for the families. Some classes make publications of poetry or other writing, class calendars, year books, and so on. I like to go to the Staten Island Ferry with my class. Some classes have end-of-the-year breakfasts or luncheons.

- Take time to honor requests for favorite poems, songs, and stories. We always reread favorite stories the last few days. Children make requests, we take a straw poll to see which ones were the favorites, and then over the last few days we read them. It's so interesting to see which stories they liked the best. It's different for every class.
- We keep most displays up on walls and bulletin board until the last possible moment, so that our room continues to have that lived-in feeling. I just can't stand looking at empty walls—it brings a cold feeling to my heart. I do begin taking down some smaller things the last full week of school. I give children photos that were posted and work that was on display. Two full days before the end of school, the children take home their journals and rainy day boxes.
- You may want to schedule a visit with teachers from the next grade (if all of your students will be promoted).
- If there are any children who will not be promoted, avoid talking to the class about "how proud your second grade teacher will be" or "how much you will love third grade." That can be very hurtful.
- On the last day of school, always a half day, we gather in a circle at story circle for Meeting. We recite favorite poems, sing favorite songs, and have a read aloud. We talk about favorite moments during the year and favorite things about first grade. That's a very special time—filled with laughter, joy, and sometimes tears. Then, suddenly, it's time for dismissal, and on to summer vacation and the future.
- Keep in mind that some of the relationships you have built with the adults and children may last for many years. So, you are not really breaking bonds with your whole class.

A group of teacher friends gather together the evening of the last day of school. We meet at one person's apartment, sit, talk, eat take-out food, and wind down. We find this ritual soothing. It's a healthy way to make the transition from the very busy last days of school to the summer. You may want to start your own ritual with colleagues, friends, or family so that you can anticipate getting (and giving) that support you may need.

In Summary

Think of yourself as a teacher-researcher as you go about becoming a teacher. Think about the constant and changing needs of your students and their families. Learn from your own positive experiences in school. Learn from your negative experiences or negative situations in your school community. Determine what *not* to do. Work closely with colleagues in your school and in the education community to find strategies and techniques that work.

There are no final solutions—be willing to continue your research. There will be difficult days. Please do not give up. If it is your dream to be an effective educator, as the poet Langston Hughes said, "Hold fast to dreams."

6

A Rich Curriculum
Is Essential

When children are involved in meaningful, hands-on, inquiry-based curriculum, discipline problems are minimized. There's just no time for fussing, whining, or other negative behavior. The children are engaged. For educators and families, there is nothing as joyous as seeing young children who are totally engaged in their work.

The Curriculum Is Interdisciplinary

The focus in our classroom is social studies, but our curriculum is interdisciplinary. For example, as part of our inquiry we interview people, do role-plays, take notes, make murals about them or the issues they discussed, write books about them, then read those books at Reading Workshop, write poems or songs about them, and so on. There may even be math or science that evolves from the interview. You can see how one interview can involve developing listening skills, acting, writing, painting, reading, singing, and so on. Because the learning involves so many different curriculum areas, it taps into the varied interests and talents of all of the students.

Self-Interest Is Critical

In an inquiry classroom you can focus on any subject area. The critical point is that the children are part of choosing the topics, asking the questions, and seeking multiple ways of finding answers. They also teach the class what they may already know about a topic. All of that involves self-interest. When children see that their issues and concerns really do matter and can become the curriculum, they will get involved.

The Learning Is Active

Inquiry studies are a very active, hands-on form of learning. The more active we make the lesson, the more the children will get involved. I have witnessed this year after year, during my thirty-one years of teaching. I have taught many, many children with serious behavior and/or learning problems, so many of whom got fully engaged in the curriculum. In fact, I love the challenge of working with such children because I get so much joy from watching them get involved.

You can read about inquiry teaching in my first two books, *Classroom Interviews: A World of Learning* and *The Research Workshop: Bringing the World into Your Classroom*. The first part of this chapter explains how an inquiry curriculum impacts on the children. We will look at how that impacts on discipline. The second part of the chapter is a brief overview of our inquiry curriculum from February to June of a recent school year.

Part 1: The Impact of the Inquiry Curriculum

In the following sections, there are observations from my experiences.

Children Want to Come to School

The children's enthusiasm starts in the morning when they wake up, eager to come to school. What a good way to start the day. What will happen at Research Workshop? What will happen at the interview? What will they see on the trip? Oh, I need to bring those bones to class for the paleontology research group.

Children Anticipate an Adventure

Once in the room, the children put the chairs at the tables, get their research journals, and form a circle where their research group will meet. Sometimes they sit around a huge piece of paper for mural making. Sometimes they sit around newspaper with a bucket of sand (with bones buried below during a study about the work of paleontologists). Sometimes they sit around newspaper with a bag of plaster, a pile of burlap strips, a pot of water for making jackets for wrapping bones. Sometimes there's a book or a pile of books to search through. Every day is an adventure. Wouldn't that make most anybody anxious to get to work and to stay involved?

Children Are Empowered by Becoming Teachers

The research begins with finding out their prior knowledge about the topic. That means that *the teacher cares about what the students already know*. They will come to see that *the teacher will involve them in teaching the other children. That is empowering.*

Children Are Empowered by Being Heard

The research continues by having the children ask questions. Those questions are recorded either by the children, one child, or by an adult. Those questions become the basis of our research. *Having someone listen to your questions and then turn those questions into the actual work of the class is empowering.*

Children Are Fascinated

The twists and turns of an inquiry study are fascinating to children (and the teachers). Who would think that they would be digging up bones, touching a real dinosaur bone right in the classroom, meeting a paleontologist, or finding out this or that? Imagine bringing Brian Pinkney to your classroom or walking into Vera B. Williams' studio as part of your research about illustrators! Imagine finding out from Akayla's grandfather that there used to be an elevated train near your school, seeing photographs of it in a book, painting a mural of it, writing a poem about it, and then bursting out with that homemade poem while sitting inside one of the real elevated trains at the Transit Museum in Brooklyn.

The Hands-On Aspect of Research Can Be So Much Fun*

Painting a mural, making concrete sidewalks, or doing a role-play is so much fun. Isn't it great to have fun? I remember so many times when the children whose behavior was seriously problematic got so involved in the hands-on aspect of our research, that visitors would never know we had such problems in our class. I recall one child, Sibby, who often fussed and refused even to sit down. But when I said, "Sibby, if you're sitting, you'll get a chance to be in the role-play," down she went.

Ivan, a child adopted from one of the horrendous orphanages of the world, was extraordinarily difficult as he adjusted to his new life in the United States. He really related to the hands-on aspect of research. He loved being in the role-plays. He loved getting his hands dirty. I could say to him, "If you want to . . . , you'll have to sit calmly and wait for your turn." Ivan would wait. Those hands-on activities were his salvation and ours, because they enabled him to be calm and to get involved.

Developing Strategies for Finding Answers to Our Questions Is Empowering

If children see that we can use books, videos, newspaper articles, the Internet, and interviews, if we can ask questions of family and friends, if we can interview people, if we can go on trips to museums, people's jobs, and other places in our quest

---

*The two names in this section are fictious, the situations were real.

to find answers—we can return to those kinds of resources to find answers to our other questions in life, both at home and at school. We are developing life-long strategies for finding answers. That is empowering. Empowerment builds self-confidence.

Our Inquiry Is Multidimensional

Every single child is involved in the research, whether it be with the whole class or in a smaller group. The role of the adults is to find those multiple ways for the children to get involved: asking questions, making observations, having deep discussions, acting in role-plays, singing songs (including ones we have written), making things, doing things, writing and then reading our homemade books, reciting poems (including ones we have written), and going places.

Our Research Is Cooperative

Children work in small or large groups. They take turns. They play different roles in the groups. They help each other. They learn from each other.

There Is an Audience

The information is shared. Each group shares its information with the whole class. It is shared orally at the end of each Research Workshop. It is shared with audiences beyond our class through murals, writing, models, poetry, skits and plays, computer contacts, and other projects. The audience includes children and adults in our school community, visitors, and often people outside of our community. Having an audience is so important.

The Families Will Know About the Inquiry

Each Monday the children take home the Family Homework bulletin, which tells about our work in each curriculum area. It tells about the issues and activities of our research groups and/or the whole class research. The homework is directly related to our research so children can anticipate their family's involvement in the inquiry.

Critical Thinking Is Expected

The children know that I really love them to think. I love it when they see connections. How do they know that? I praise them. "That was brilliant. Tell the class again." "Unbelievable. That was amazing thinking. I'm going to tell your parents." "Fantastic. Would you go and tell Isabel (kindergarten teacher) what you just said."

You might say that these are young children, and you may wonder what I'm talking about when I say they think deeply. Young children can be profound. They can be deep thinkers. Just ask any early childhood teacher who loves teaching. Some children whose behavior may be regarded as problematic have been through experiences that enable them to have a deeper understanding about life. When such children know that you treasure their insights, they will engage in that hard work of thinking.

When children know their thinking is valued, they think even more, even deeper. They look for meaning in events. They may see connections between concepts in books we have read—"That innkeeper (in *Peter and the North Wind*) reminds me of the Bumba in *Akimba and the Magic Cow*." They may see connections between events in history—when they learned that Alvin Ailey wasn't allowed to attend dance school, someone said, "Isn't that what happened to Bessie Coleman when she wanted to become a pilot?" They may see connections between happenings in science—"Look, the water in our concrete evaporated just like what happened to the water on the slate board."

Children's Behavior Has a Lot to Do with Expectations

My students know that the adults expect them to participate in our activities. At the start of Research Workshop, for example, they know that they must get their research materials, sit with their research journals open, and have a pencil handy. Before we start an interview, they know they must have their interview journal and a pencil handy and copy the person's name and the date from the dry mark board. They know that at Math Workshop, they are expected to help make a circle of children big enough for all of the children in the group to fit comfortably.

The children know they will be called on to participate in many ways. They know they can't just sit back and do nothing or fool around. It just can't happen. That's easier said than done. The role of the teacher is to enable the children to see what is expected of them through her comments and actions. The children know their families will learn about the research and will also expect them to participate. The children rise to the occasion.

Part 2: A Brief Overview of Our Inquiry Curriculum from February to June

If you have read my previous books, the research topics in this section will be familiar, but the content and activities vary because they are based on the children's questions and the available resources (including interviews).

Research About the Work of Paleontologists

From September through January, our class had done research about a block on Second Avenue near our school. We had looked at the block today and in "the olden days." We were about to launch our People at Work research in February. The children made a list of jobs they wanted to study. The long list included these and other topics: health care workers (many of the children's parents are health care workers), dancers, singers, jugglers (Lena's father is a professional juggler), paleontologists (Jake and Noah are avid dinosaur enthusiasts), and child labor (Chandra's friend and Allison's brother had been in previous classes where we had done research about child labor).

After a straw poll we decided to focus on two topics for now, and the child labor study would come later in the year. One group would do research with Dolores Buonasora, a teaching assistant, and me about health care workers. The other group would do research about paleontologists with our student teacher, Esther Nuñez, a senior at New York University, and with Petrana Koutcheva, a paraprofessional who was assigned to work with a special needs child.

In their effort to answer their questions, Esther and Petrana's group followed paleontology expeditions to all parts of the world using books from the public library. They "traveled" to Madagascar, Mongolia, Montana, and elsewhere by "planes" and "trains," and "cars," depending on the location. They replicated the work of the paleontologists in the books—digging up bones hidden in buckets of sand or soil using the same kinds of tools—awls, toothbrushes, and shovels. They wrapped the bones (from chickens, cows, fish, and pigs—all brought from home) using burlap dipped in plaster. What a delightful mess. They recorded information in their journals about the location of the bones, the answers to their questions, and so on.

As they worked, they discussed the issues faced by paleontologists—how to get to the bones, how to preserve the bones so they could get them safely to the lab, what to do with the bones after they finished studying them, and so on. These were some of the questions the children had asked on the first day of their research. They also asked whether they should keep the bones for themselves as was done in the old days or return them to the country or state of origin, as has been done in recent years.

Esther and Petrana's group focused for a few weeks on the book, *Digging for Bird Dinosaurs: An Expedition to Madagascar*, by Nic Bishop, which was about an expedition to Madagascar, off the coast of southern Africa. The expedition was led by Cathy Forster and a group of paleontologists from SUNY Stony Brook, a New York State college in Long Island. It was amazing to see how well that book suited our hands-on research style. It seemed like the perfect book to answer the children's questions as well as raise new questions and issues for discussion.

The work done each day by the paleontologist research group was shared with the whole class. Children who were not in that group but who wanted to try digging for bones, wrapping bones, and so on, had a chance to do that at Center Time. All interviews and trips involved the whole class.

Our class went on a trip to the Museum of Natural History, which was just across Central Park from our school. Lena's second cousin, Bev, works with volunteers at the museum, so she took time from her work to guide us around. In one of the vast rooms of dinosaur exhibits, a volunteer let us touch bones and answered an open spigot of questions from the children and the parents who accompanied us. In another room, there was a replica of a paleontology dig—it looked so much like what we had done in class. There were the same awls, toothbrushes, and other tools, as well as the bones and the jackets.

Children squealed with glee when we saw on the TV monitor above the famous paleontologist, Dr. Mark Norel, whom we had read about in a *New York Times* article. (They felt as if they knew him just because we read about him.) "There's Mark Norel. We know him!" The article was about recent research in Mongolia where the paleontologists have concluded, in consultation with Mark Norel and others around the world, that dinosaurs were indeed related to birds.

After I found that article in the *New York Times*, the paleontologist group had discussed it. Then, during Share Time, we had a whole class discussion. "What is this consultation?" we wondered together. We role-played paleontologists consulting. "How would you consult with someone all the way in Mongolia?" I asked as we looked at the map. "Email, telephone, letters, visits," said various students, some of whom were well aware of the sophisticated technology. (Later, at interviews of health care workers, we would revisit the concept of consultation.) Bev informed us that Mark was present in the museum that day, but he was just too busy for us to see him. (A subsequent year, we did get to interview Mark Norel.)

The children compared the work of paleontologists in the different expeditions—their goals, their means of travel, their tools, and so on. On a day when Esther was not in class, the whole class replicated the expedition to Mongolia, as it was presented in the book *Searching for Velociraptor*, by Lowell Dingus in consultation with Mark Norel.

On that last day of their expedition, when one of the paleontologists finally stumbled on the bones of the great velociraptor, we replicated that scene. Our paleontologist rushed back to the camp to tell his colleagues. They hurried back to the sight and, in panic mode, wrapped the bones, hoping to finish before dark so they could bring the treasured bones back to the United States. We, too, rushed and wrapped the bones in burlap dipped in plaster. When our actors depicted the excitement of those moments, it seemed so dull to me. I took over the role-play and shouted with enthusiasm, "Look, it's a velociraptor!!!!" When we redid the role-play, the children also shouted with great fervor.

Later, at Writing Workshop, that moment when they found the velociraptor bones became Matthew's new poem. A group of children worked at Center Time to paint a mural about Matthew's poem. We painted his poem right into the mural. The mural hung in a prominent location in our room until the last week of school when Matthew took it home.

The whole class saw a National Geographic video about that same expedition to Mongolia. We watched the paleontologists as they traveled in jeeps across the Gobi Desert, as they searched for bones from an early era, as they made their finds, as they wrapped the bones, as they camped under the stars.

You can read about the high point of the research about paleontologists in Chapter 7, where I describe the interview of paleontologists Cathy Forster and Jim Clark, which happened right in our classroom. Our culminating activity was a splendid paleontology luncheon on the day of that interview.

This research involved so many curriculum areas:

reading—nonfiction books, magazines, information on the Internet, instructions, captions in books, labels on murals, paleontology poems

science—asking and answering questions about the science and work of paleontologists, replicating the work of scientists, learning about evaporation (in the work with plaster), thinking critically

writing—taking notes, writing poems as well as fiction and nonfiction, making labels for murals

math—developing skills such as classification, counting, solving word problems, thinking about sizes and shapes, questions about time, patterns (such as the similarities of work in different expeditions)

social studies—working with maps, discussing concepts about work, raising ethical issues about paleontology (returning bones to the place or country of origin), engaging in social action

art—painting murals, making drawings, using plaster, making dinosaur models

Also, there was a tremendous amount of *family involvement*: sending in resources (books, videos, bones, pictures, tools), going on the class trip, working with their children on related homework assignments, cooking for and attending the luncheon for the paleontologists.

Research About the Work of Health Care Workers

It was unusual to have so many family members who were health care workers. No wonder so many children wanted to get involved in this inquiry study. Some had visited their parents at work and had lots of background knowledge. However, some children whose parents were health care workers knew almost nothing about their parents' work. The list of questions generated by the children was gigantic. In the process of answering their questions, my research group and the whole class did so many things. Here are just a few:

A HOSPITAL

We took over the block area and set up a hospital in the classroom. Families sent in supplies. Children used the hospital daily at Center Time. As we learned more and more, we added to activities at the hospital. The children wore lab coats and used each other or dolls as patients. It was a very popular hospital.

ELIZABETH BLACKWELL

We learned about Elizabeth Blackwell in our quest to find out about how women first became doctors in the United States. We role-played her story as we did the research. We painted and labeled a mural about her.

INTERVIEWS

The whole class had many interviews. During the interviews children asked questions, took notes in their interview journals, participated in role-plays, and participated in discussions. Each interview generated concepts and issues to think about. We interviewed these parents about their work:

Hayden's father, Larry, a heart specialist
Andrew's father, Steve, a massage therapist, and his mother, Margot, a midwife
Laura's mother, Consuelo, a health care researcher doing research about strokes
Allison's mother, Alyse, the Deputy Commissioner of Health in a local town
James' father, Paul, a gastroenterologist, and his mother, Leza, a pathologist
(who came for a second interview about her lobbying work in Washington, D.C.). Each child got to see cells from their own cheeks under a microscope.
Katie's mother, Kathy, a dialysis nurse
Rani's father, Omar, a nurse, administrator, and specialist in CPR
Mahalah's father, Mitch, a geriatric psychologist
Sabrina's mother, Lisa, a pediatric psychologist

In addition, we interviewed a friend of one of the families, Dr. Julie Luttinger, a pediatrician. We painted a mural about Julie. We interviewed the MNS nurse, Judy.

When I worked in a low-income neighborhood, we had just as many family members who were health care workers at a local hospital.

HOMEMADE BOOKS

For each interview each child wrote and illustrated a page for a homemade book. Each of these many homemade books was used for word study two or three days per week at Reading Workshop. The books were also sent home for the children to read and discuss with their families.

TRIPS

We walked to Hayden's father's office. We took a school bus to Local 1199 of the Health Care Worker's Union.

FIRST-HAND LEARNING

We learned first-hand about childhood diabetes when a member of our class was diagnosed with this illness. Children watched their classmate give herself regular blood tests. They took her to the nurse when necessary.

BOOKS

We searched through nonfiction books. We read fiction such as Tomie dePaola's *Now One Foot, Now the Other*. The grandfather in this touching story had a stroke. During our block study in the beginning of the year, we interviewed a man who had had a stroke.

Many children did extra credit research at home about health care workers who work with people or animals. They presented their oral and written reports to the class.

FAMILY INVOLVEMENT

There was a lot of family involvement: sending in resources, coming for or arranging interviews, joining our class for trips, working with their children on related homework assignments.

Research About Child Labor and Sweatshops

Our student teacher had completed her placement, so the whole class worked together. The children asked many questions that became the focus of our research. Here are some of the activities. Over the course of one month, we:

- looked at many photographs and read many labels of photographs about child labor
- read and discussed fiction and historical fiction
- did many role-plays based on real-life current situations we learned about from the newspaper or Internet reports
- watched videos about child labor
- interviewed these people: Somini Sengupta, a journalist from the *New York Times*, who told us about how and why she wrote an article about young

children who were taken from Bangladesh to become camel jockeys in the United Arab Emirates. This interview was arranged by Jake's mother, Susan. Matthew's mother, Ione, talked about child labor in her country, Brazil.

- wrote pages for the homemade books about each interview
- did word study using the homemade books. The children read and discussed the books with their families.
- painted murals about the camel jockeys and about child labor in Brazil
- wrote many poems and stories about child labor
- wrote our own play, including a poem and a song, about our research. There were scenes about the camel jockeys, children picking coffee beans in Brazil, and young women making clothes in Bangladesh. The children spoke in Bengali, Arabic, Portuguese, and English. We presented this play, camels and all, to more than 125 family members and friends at the Family Celebration in mid-June.
- rejoiced during the summer to read in the newspaper that the practice of taking the young children to be camel jockeys is now banned and several mechanisms for enforcement are being put into place!

In Summary

This curriculum hardly sounds like a first grade curriculum. It certainly does not conform to the standard first grade social studies curriculum recommended by the Board of Education. I simply stretched the standard curriculum about community helpers (police, fire fighters, letter carriers) to include other workers. In the process, the children developed skills in all curriculum areas, and they loved doing it. Such a curriculum changes the nature of classroom management.

7

Interviews Can Help Develop Values

Our class dives right into our research the first day of school. By the second or third day of school, we have our first research-related interview. When we did research about a block on Second Avenue for six months during one school year, I looked right away at the addresses of the family to see if anyone lived on or near that block. On that first day, I asked Chandra's mother, Colette Hughes, if she would come for an interview the next day at 9:00 A.M. Fortunately, Colette was able to arrange her work around my request.

Before the class entered the room on that second day of school, I told the children to look in their cubbies for the brown interview journal, get a pencil from the pencil containers, and come to story circle. By providing lots of support, we had a successful and delightful first interview of Chandra's mother, Colette.

Little by little, the children approximated interview skills until they were quite adept at interviewing people. There are a number of skills that they developed over time, some were just behavioral and others were academic skills. Here are some of those skills:

- bringing the interview journal and pencil to story circle
- finding a seat on the carpet and then copying the date and the name of the person to be interviewed without being told by the teacher
- taking initiative to raise your hand and ask questions
- listening to the questions and the answers
- saying that you don't understand something
- participating in or watching role-plays
- thinking
- participating in discussions with the person next to you and with the whole class

- thinking about what information to record in the journal and how to record it
- using the skills at hand (pictures, approximated spelling, using words from the classroom environment) to record information
- sitting relatively still without blocking the view of the person behind you
- thinking about what to write for the homemade book; writing that and drawing an illustration

That's a lot of work for a six- or seven-year-old child. It was amazing to see the very active participation in the interviews, which ranged from one-half hour to an hour and one-half. Of course, it's the teacher's responsibility to help the children understand and to make the interview interesting. I'm always checking to see if children understand what is being said. I'm always thinking about role-plays, both to help children understand and to promote a more active form of learning. You can read more about interviews in *Classroom Interviews: A World of Learning* (Rogovin 1998).

How Are Behavior and Interviews Connected?

There's a lot of discipline involved in participating in an interview. There is, of course, the discipline noted above—the sitting, following the guidelines such as raising one's hand, and so on. But, there is the larger concept of behavior—one's behavior as a human being. I want to promote values such as caring, fairness, justice, cooperation, and peace. Yes, I want the children to care about these issues in the world outside our classroom. These are the same values I want to see applied in the classroom and in the school yard. I want to develop a caring, fair, just, cooperative, and peaceful classroom community.

But how are behavior and interviews connected? Interviews make information easily accessible to children. Our interviews may be about someone's hobby or job, someone's culture, or someone's life. Interviews are special because they give us a window into people's thoughts, values, hopes, and dreams. Interviews present an opportunity for children to learn these values from the adults around them. The adults can serve as role models. Sometimes we see these values when they talk about their work or their lives outside of work. Sometimes the values are quite apparent. Sometimes they are hidden like little gems inside the interview. It is up to the teacher and/or the children to uncover these treasures.

How Can We Make Interviews More Than Just an Exchange of Information?

Our role as educators is to create an atmosphere in the classroom where the person being interviewed as well as the children are comfortable. If we are particularly interested in developing values and seeing the person as a role model or inspiration, we have to work at it.

Listen for Gems About Values

Listen for gems. These are the things a person may say (casually or deliberately) or do about values or human character. Think of how and when to talk about them with the children. When Nora Guthrie talked about how her father, Woody, gave his new coat to a stranger who was cold, I knew we had a gem. Right then and there, we had a discussion about how important this was. Days later, we completed a mural of Woody giving his coat to a stranger.

Sometimes a person talks and talks at the interview. Just listen. Don't stop to explain everything to the children. Just wait until you hear something in all that talk, something that is a significant concept or piece of information for the children or something that shows the person's character. It's a little like sifting the rocks for gold nuggets.

Nurture these gems throughout the school year by:

- making a mural or poster
- writing poetry or stories
- writing a song
- writing and producing a play

Listen for Gems in Various Curriculum Areas

Embedded in nearly every interview is something that has the potential for learning in science, social studies, math, reading, writing, art, or music. Listen carefully for that. You may decide to discuss these topics at the interview or to bring them up at a later date.

Find Out More About the Person You Are Interviewing

Sometimes I talk with the person ahead of time, or sometimes we chat quietly while the children are taking notes. When I want to share what I have learned from the person, either I have a child ask or I will ask about some other aspect of the person's life that I predict will be significant to the children. I did this at the interview of James' grandfather, Morris, when I had the children ask what it was like to be hungry. Also, I asked Morris to tell us about polishing shoes during the Depression. I knew something special would come from that.

Change the Direction of the Interview If Necessary

When we interviewed Dora Cruz about Puerto Rico during a cultural study, I thought that what she said about taking care of her sick mother was far more significant than the information about Puerto Rico. We focused the rest of the interview on her mother. You can read about that interview in *Classroom Interviews*. By the way, Dora became a teaching assistant in my class as well as a very important worker in the after school center.

Let the Person Know That You Value Them

When Bobby De Cola, a sanitation worker, came for an interview, he was touched by how he was treated by the children and me. We talked about how important his work was for the city. He talked about his most important job, which was to be a father. Bobby cried when we gave him the homemade book about him. He even came to our Family Celebrations with his daughter.

When we interviewed Anthony, a worker from Ready, Willing, and Able, part of the Doe Foundation that helps people who have been homeless or out of work, Anthony was moved by our respect for him. At one point in the interview, he explained the science of why he stops watering the trees in October. He spoke so patiently and thoughtfully. I turned to him and told him that he sounded like a real teacher the way he explained the concepts. He whispered to me later that in his earlier life, he had worked with children. When people see that you value them, they will open up and tell you more. They may invite you to their work. They may join you at events later in the year.

Bring the Person and the Issues They Raised into Other Conversations

All through the year, we recall what someone said, just as we recall important concepts from literature or our research. A child said, "Gee, Morris is like the good daughter in *Mufaro's Beautiful Daughter*." I asked why she thought that. Then I complimented the child for seeing that connection.

After we interviewed Hayden's father, Larry Hecker, about his job as a surgeon, one of the big things we remembered and talked about from that interview was that Larry thought it was so important to make his patients feel comfortable. He made our class feel comfortable at his office. We talked over and over at various times during the year about how he was so respectful to the people who worked for him.

Search for Ways to Involve Families

For the first six months of the school year, our class was doing research about a block on Second Avenue, between 83rd and 84th Streets. As we were planning the research, I thought about each student and their family:

How could we involve different families?
Which of our class families were not very involved in our school?
Which families needed to be drawn into our curriculum?
Whom could we interview?
How could we involve a family in order to boost a child's self-esteem?

How could we do this through our research about the block on Second Avenue (or any other research topic)?

Interview—Nikola Curovic, Tommy's Father, Building Superintendent

It was very important to me, in terms of bringing Tommy's family into the class-room community, to arrange an interview very early in the school year. Of course, there were building superintendents in each of the buildings on Second Avenue on the block we were studying. But, instead of interviewing a superintendent on Second Avenue, we went to Tommy's building on 84th Street to interview Nikola, also known as Nick.

The day before the interview I drew a map of our neighborhood, showing our school, Tommy's block, and our block on Second Avenue. I asked the kids why we would want to interview Nick who didn't even work on Second Avenue. The answers evolved quickly. The work of supers was probably similar, so it would be okay to learn from a super who was not on Second Avenue.

Nick greeted us with a warm, very friendly hello. Then he took us on a tour of his apartment building. We went right into the hot boiler room, where he showed us his two mighty boilers and described how they heated the building—a great science lesson for another day. We went to the parking garage where we saw a kind of tractor Nick used for carrying the garbage and recycling. We even went to Tommy's apartment where we saw Tommy's mother, Rosa, and Mark, one of Tommy's two older brothers. Nick and Rosa were touched by our visit. And it brought them right into the center of our classroom community.

Expanding Beyond the Interview

This particular interview had the potential for expanding into other curriculum areas.

READING AND WRITING

The next day, the children each wrote a page for our homemade book about Nick. A few weeks later, that book became our guided reading for two days. During word study with the book, we found lots of words that had the same *oi* spelling as the word *boiler*. We looked at other words with the *ck* as in *Nick's* name: *tick, tick tock, luck, lock, backpack, neck,* and more. Imagine, your family being the reading lesson for your class? Imagine what that can do for your self-esteem.

Our class loved poetry. Every day at Meeting we recited poems, almost as if they were music. Shortly after the trip to Tommy's house, I suggested we write a poem together about Nick. As children suggested words or phrases, I quickly jotted them down in a journal. I selected some of their words and phrases, and we fashioned them into a poem. With a few adjustments after school, we had our poem.

> **Tommy's Father Nick,**
> Oh no.
> the water's leaking on my head,
> on my bed,
> on the floor,
> out the door.
> Let's call Nick.
> Hello Nick, this is apartment 407.
> The water's leaking on our heads,
> on our bed,
> on the floor,
> out the door.
> Help Nick, please help!
> "Okay, here I come."
> It was 12 o'clock midnight.
> What a sight.
> Nick fixed that pipe.
> Thanks Nick,
> You're great.
> You're a really super Super.
>
> *by class 1-407*

I copied that poem onto poster board and laminated it so that we could add it to our collection of favorite poems by such great poets as Langston Hughes, Marilyn Singer, Issa, Eloise Greenfield, and Monica Gunning, and Lynn Joseph, all marvelous writers of poetry for children. Tommy recited the part of his father every time we recited that poem, even at our huge Family Celebration at night in November. Just imagine how Tommy felt as we recited that poem right up to the last day of school.

In addition to the poem we wrote together and the pages for the homemade book, several children wrote books about Nick and about the boiler during Writing Workshop. This kept those special thoughts about Nick alive in our classroom.

SCIENCE

If a teacher is on the lookout, she can often find science embedded in an interview. The interview of Nick was filled with potential science lessons: boiling water to make steam, oil, heat rising, pipes coming into a building from the street, and so on. We were thrilled to see the pipes in the basement of Tommy's building because it helped us answer one of our questions about how water came into buildings on the block we were studying. Also, we saw the pipes that took water from the boiler up into the rest of Tommy's building. At home, for extra credit, children worked with their families to boil water and watch the steam rise.

SOCIAL STUDIES

As the children interviewed Nick and toured his building, they learned about the very important work of a superintendent. They could use that information to help them understand the work of supers on Second Avenue. They could see this work as valuable in our society.

ART

Within days of the trip to Tommy's house, a group of children worked with me to paint a mural of Nick in the boiler room, our favorite part of the trip. That mural, along with photos of our trip, hung right near our rocking chair at story circle. Of course, nearly everyone who came into our room for the rest of the year got to see the mural and hear our poem.

What Does This Interview Have to Do with Behavior and Values?

FEELING GOOD ABOUT ONESELF

Behavior and self-esteem are interrelated. The trip, the poem, the homemade book, and the mural were all part of a deliberate effort to help Tommy feel good about himself and his family. And he did.

HELPING A FAMILY FEEL WELCOME AND COMFORTABLE

By getting Tommy's family involved in our curriculum, they felt good about his school experience. Nick now greeted me with a morning hug and a friendly hello. Rosa and I talked frequently in the playground after school. She told me she felt welcome and comfortable and that Tommy was so happy to come to school. I got to learn more about Tommy. Rosa began to have Tommy read with her and do the Family Homework on the weekend. This was an adjustment I made when I saw that parents were not really available to help a child during the work week. Usually the homework was due on Friday. I learned that Tommy stayed up very late because his mother was at work, and he hung out with his two older brothers. All of the discussions with Nick, Rosa, and the brothers informed my teaching.

TAKING PRIDE IN ONE'S WORK

Previously the children hadn't really noticed Nick. Now he was a superstar and a friend to the children. The way Nick presented his work to us was a great inspiration to the children. Here was someone who talked with joy about being helpful to the people in his building and in the neighborhood. In fact, Nick was our teacher, too. I wanted the children to see that the work of a building superintendent was just as important as that of a doctor or a teacher. This was an important value I wanted to develop in our classroom community.

FAMILIES HELPING THE CLASS IN DIFFERENT WAYS

We knew we could turn to Nick to do a few small repairs for our class. He fixed the knob on our clock and the special easel with a sign that welcomes people to the fourth floor. He did that work with great pride. Tommy just glowed with pride.

FRIENDSHIP AND BONDING

All of this enabled Tommy to feel good about coming to school. He began to focus more on his work and made a lot of progress. He began to speak up and to participate in the classroom research and in discussions. He began to ask questions. Then Tommy made friends in class. They had a continuous game of tag in the play yard at recess and after school. Nick and Rosa watched with great pride as Tommy participated in the class play we wrote and presented in June, a play about child labor.

FUNCTIONING AT AN INTERVIEW

Sitting and participating fully at an interview is a very important skill. It requires discipline—sitting relatively still for an extended period of time, sitting so others behind you can see, listening to questions and answers, taking notes, participating in role-plays, and processing a whole lot of ideas and information. At each interview, the children develop these skills.

Interview—Morris Basuk, James' Grandfather

At The Manhattan New School there is a tradition of inviting grandparents, other family members, or other special people to visit right after the Thanksgiving weekend. On Special People's Day we had several grandparents in our classroom. This was just perfect because we were doing research about our block on Second Avenue. We had moved from looking at the block as it is today to looking at it in the old days. We wanted to know about the music, the games and toys, the sports, the schools, the clothes, and more. The children wanted to know when people on the block first got TVs, VCRs, radios, lights, and other things that used electricity. On Special People's Day, the grandparents were bursting with things to tell us about the old days. After a while, it got so informal that Jake's grandfather and James' grandparents were having a grand conversation, and we were just listening.

I was listening for two things. First, I wanted to make sure the children understood what the grandparents were saying. Every once in a while, I interjected to help clarify a concept. Secondly, I was listening for gems—perhaps something that might warrant bringing one of the grandparents back for a full interview, perhaps something we could follow up on in class—it could have been some information, a concept, or a value. Something in what James' grandfather, Morris, said told me we just had to bring him back for an interview.

Morris mentioned that during the Great Depression he used to shine shoes. I didn't stop that day to have him explain. We needed more time with Morris. This lively, shockingly white-haired grandfather in his eighties was delighted to come back for an interview. Before I arrived at story circle where the children sat with journals in hand, and where Morris sat in the rocking chair, a conversation had already started. When I arrived and sat on my chair, Morris was saying, "I love books. Books are my friends. When I see a book, I just want to kiss it." Just then, Morris saw a pile of copies of Else Holmelund Minarik's book, *A Kiss for Little Bear*. As if in shock, he said, "I just said I could kiss the books, and now I see a book called *A Kiss for Little Bear*. That's amazing." The children never forgot that. That incident came up over and over during the year. It really touched our hearts. What an inspiration.

The children asked Morris lots of questions about New York in the old days. But, I remembered what he had said about shining shoes on Special People's Day. I asked the children to ask Morris about when he used to shine shoes in the old days. Briefly he told about the Great Depression, when millions of people had lost their jobs. At age nine, Morris had to get a job shining shoes because his father couldn't find a job, so he had to shine shoes. Morris proceeded to role-play shining my shoes. I happened to have a can of shoe polish (from some past study). Oh, he was working full speed, pretending to shine my shoes, and talking all the while. It was splendid.

Again I was listening carefully, as teachers need to do during interviews. What was Morris saying that would be important for the children? After all, he was saying a whole lot, more than they could possibly absorb. I then said, "Morris, you mentioned before that you were hungry during the Depression. What was it like to be hungry?" Morris told how his stomach used to hurt when he was hungry. He used to drink lots of water to fill his stomach. Then, in true Morris style, he exclaimed, "Boys and girls, did you know that every minute more than 3,000 children around the world die of hunger?" He told them that this was terrible, and that we must do something about it. I just wanted to hug Morris for bringing these issues into our classroom in such an impassioned way.

Expanding Beyond the Interview

Creating Meaningful Writing and Reading Experiences and Topics

After Morris left, the children wrote their pages for the homemade book. We revisited the interview a few weeks later when we did word study with the book about Morris during Reading Workshop. Again there were discussions about the issues Morris raised.

We posted photographs of Morris in the classroom and the hallway. Children wrote labels for the photographs. We kept his spirit alive.

BRINGING OUR WORK INTO THE CHILDREN'S HOMES

The week after the interview, I talked with the families through the Family Homework about the central issues from Morris' interview. I asked them to read the homemade book and to discuss this interview with their children. Here was another chance to revisit the interview. Some grandparents told children of their family's experiences during the Great Depression.

What Did This Interview Have to Do with Behavior and Values?

FINDING A ROLE MODEL

A family member or a teacher can tell a child how important reading is for them. How much more it means when someone bursts in as Morris did to tell children that books are our friends—what a role model. How much more it means when a friendly grandfather talks about the importance of fighting against world hunger. A skeptic may question how that could really affect a child's behavior or schoolwork. It can.

ENGAGING IN SOCIAL ACTION

Morris helped the children become more socially conscious. Even though our research was not about hunger, as Morris had suggested and as we had done in other years, we did get involved later in the year in social action dealing with the issues of child labor.

CREATING AN ATMOSPHERE

Statements like those that Morris made about books and reading help build an atmosphere, an ambiance, a feeling, a love of books in the classroom. In kids' words, "Reading is cool." Identifying reading as "cool" can make a big difference for children. In some households reading is no big deal, it's not so important, or it's "uncool." A visitor like Morris can actually turn a child's thinking around. With the whole class getting excited about what Morris said, it's something like adding healthy vegetables and delicious herbs and spices to the soup simmering in the pot.

BUILDING GENERATIONS INTO THE CLASSROOM

Some children don't have grandparents or older people in their lives. Bringing people into the classroom community from an older generation is important. Often, it feels so good. And, their messages are often heard in a different way than the messages of parents. For many years I have had senior citizens reading weekly with my children. One woman who was in her late eighties could hardly hear what the children were reading, but the love and kindness and concern meant so much to the children I had selected to read to her. Sometimes that just makes the difference and can influence how seriously a child will take his work.

REMEMBERING OUR ROLE MODELS THROUGHOUT THE YEAR

Morris returned to our classroom for the paleontology luncheon and for our Family Celebration. Everyone was so happy to see him. He was already part of our classroom family.

Interview—Zada Abdalrhman, Rani's Mother

In that same block study about Second Avenue, the children wanted to know about the people who lived on the block. It happened that there were people of many backgrounds, something so wonderful about New York City. (Unfortunately, so many towns and cities are so segregated that you simply can't meet such a variety of people.) As we did our research, we found out that there were people from all over the world who lived on our block.

In the aftermath of the tragedy at the World Trade Center (which was in the southern part of our school district), anti-Arab, anti-Muslim sentiment was taking over the news. I had even heard it from one child in my classroom. Zada and her friends had already felt the sting of that prejudice in the city. I wanted to find ways to counteract that prejudice in a way that would be supportive to the three Muslim families in our class. So, as part of meeting people on the block who were of different backgrounds, I decided we should ask Rani's mother, Zada, to come for an interview. I knew that getting to know Zada and her husband Omar (a nurse) would be so important. (We would interview Omar later in the year as part of our research about health care workers.) Zada, a most warm and delightful person, is a Muslim and lived most of her life in Haifa, Israel. She taught us some Arabic, which we wove into a poem about her a few weeks later.

When she arrived at the interview, Zada had olive oil from the olive trees in her mother's yard in Israel, as well as the other ingredients for making hummus and tahini. As the blender whirled, Zada kept answering our questions. The children (who are often so finicky about trying new foods) surprised us by asking for seconds and thirds.

Zada was really good at playing a rock game—similar to but different from the rock games played by Nalina, from India, and Jeongsook, from Korea, and Petrana, from Bulgaria (who worked in our classroom), all of whom we had interviewed earlier. We actually had a friendly rock game competition at our Family Celebration in November—where all the adults who had played a rock game in their childhood came up on the stage to play. It was great fun.

Expanding Beyond the Interview

WRITING ABOUT A SPECIFIC TOPIC

There is a discipline involved in thinking through a whole interview, and then deciding what to write on your page for the homemade book. Some children selected one aspect of the interview—the food, the rock game, the Arabic words, and so on. Others chose to summarize the interview.

DOING WORD STUDY

Word study is a marvelous time in our class. It's a great example of cooperative learning. Before we gather, I remind the children to bring their reading journals and pencils. A child took over my job and asked, "What do you predict will be in this book about Zada?" Our lesson flows directly from their predictions. Because I use this as an opportunity to develop handwriting skills, we sound out the letters of a word that was predicted, and then the children copy the letters from the dry mark board. I choose to do word study with certain of the words they predict. For example, if a child suggests that *cook* would be in the book about Zada, I may decide to have the class think of other words that have *oo* as in *cook*. I may give clues for words: I'm thinking of a word that is something you read. I'm thinking of something we hang our coats on. Some children suggest other words. We add them to our list on the board. If a child suggests *mood*, because it has the *oo*, we will put that word in a box on the board and talk about why it is different from the *oo* in cook. It has the right spelling but a different sound. During word study, children are bursting with predictions, words with similar sounds or spellings, and observations. There is often laughter. It's rigorous, and it's so much fun that the children hardly recognize the fact that we are working so hard.

What Did This Interview Have to Do with Behavior and Values?

REDUCING PREJUDICE

Getting to know people of different backgrounds from our own is an important part of reducing prejudice. The children were learning Arabic and eating Arabic foods. For most of the children, it was the first time they met someone who said they were of the Muslim faith (although we had three Muslim families in our class). Also, both Zada and Omar taught us so much about our research topics. Here were two wonderful, intelligent, friendly people, right in our midst. What great role models. And, in our own small world of the classroom, we helped counteract prejudice and build understanding.

BUILDING SELF-ESTEEM

Rani was just learning English, while the other children were fluent. He worked extremely hard in class and at home. Rani was so incredibly proud of his parents when they came for the interviews. These interviews were so important for his self-esteem.

LEARNING FROM OTHERS

Families read about Zada and Omar in the Family Homework and in the home-made books about the interviews. As parents got to know them, there was an increase in playdates (kids getting together outside of school). Rani and the other children learned a lot of each other's families.

Interview—Julie Luttinger, Pediatrician, Friend of Emma's Family

During the second part of the school year, the children chose to do research about health care workers. We happened to have lots of parents who were health care workers, so, week after week, we interviewed these parents. Then Emma Brecher's mother, Ellen, asked me if I would like her to arrange an interview of Julie, a young, female doctor she knew. Ellen had been talking with Julie about our health care research, when Julie told her a marvelous story. When Julie was in third grade, her mother sat her down and asked her what she wanted to be when she grew up. Julie talked about being a teacher or a nurse, one of those women-friendly professions. Her mother handed her a book about Elizabeth Blackwell, the first woman doctor in the United States. Wow! I knew we had to interview Julie because we had already done research about Elizabeth Blackwell. In fact, we had read a book about Elizabeth Blackwell, done numerous role-plays, and had even painted a large mural that was hanging in our room surrounded by lots of signs telling about Elizabeth's life. We had read that book in answer to a question I had posed to the children in my research group, "We keep seeing that there were no women doctors in the old days. How did we get from having no women doctors to having many women doctors today?"

So, Ellen arranged the interview. Julie answered many questions about her work. I waited patiently for someone to ask her *why* she wanted to be a doctor. When she started to tell her story about Elizabeth Blackwell, the children just burst! "We know about Elizabeth Blackwell." You should have seen the expressions on their faces. Here was a real person, a real doctor who had been inspired by someone we read about in a book. That really validated our research. And, it served as an inspiration to the children.

Expanding Beyond the Interview

WRITING, ART, AND READING

That day, the children drew pictures as they wrote pages for the homemade book about Julie. A few weeks later we did word study with that homemade book. The children took their copies home and read and discussed them with their families. That sparked numerous discussions at home.

At Center Time, a group of children worked with me on a two-part mural about Julie. The first part showed her as a child sitting in a chair and her mother handing her the book (which happened to be the exact same book we had read) about Elizabeth Blackwell. The second part was a life-size picture of Julie. Children wrote signs explaining the mural. We hung it right next to the mural about Elizabeth Blackwell. At the end of the year Emma gave the mural to Julie. Julie even came to our Family Celebration in June.

What Did This Interview Have to Do with Behavior and Values?

ENGAGING CHILDREN IN MEANINGFUL WORK THAT KEEPS CHILDREN FOCUSED

The children were deeply engaged in the research about Elizabeth Blackwell and were totally involved in the interview, the homemade book, and the mural about Julie. When children are deeply engaged in their work, they are focused. Fooling around or daydreaming is rare.

FEELING GOOD ABOUT ONESELF

Emma felt so good that her mother had arranged the interview with Julie, and that Julie now meant so much to our class. That experience was important for Emma's self-esteem. Feeling good about oneself is critical. Emma participated even more in class and made great progress.

FINDING ROLE MODELS TO INSPIRE CHILDREN

Both Elizabeth Blackwell and Julie Luttinger served as role models and an inspiration for the whole class, not just for the girls. It wasn't at all easy for Elizabeth to become a doctor—she was rejected from twenty-nine medical schools. When she finally went to medical school, she was shunned by the male students and people in the town. She served as an example of someone who fought for her dream to come true. She reminded the children of the words, "Hold fast to dreams," in Langston Hughes' poem, "Dreams."

INVOLVING THE FAMILIES

Emma was new in our school. It was important to Emma's mother that I had honored her suggestion about interviewing Julie. This was the second time that we interviewed people she had recommended. This gave Ellen confidence that I really did view the families as my colleagues, that I really wanted their involvement. Having confidence in your child's teacher has a direct impact on a child's participation in class.

Interview—Cathy Forster and Jim Clark, Paleontologists

In Chapter 6, you can read about our research about the work of paleontologists. The climax of our research was when Cathy Forster and Jim Clark came in from

Long Island for an interview. We had read about Cathy in *Digging for Bird Dinosaurs: An Expedition to Madagascar* and about Jim in *Searching for Velociraptor*. Sylvie Edmonds' mother, Margo, took my challenge to the families and used the Internet to track down Cathy at SUNY Stony Brook. Cathy happily accepted.

The children had seen another library book that listed famous paleontologists. Cathy was in that book, too. We read with excitement that Cathy had decided at age three to become a paleontologist when her parents gave her a toy Brontosaurus she named "Bronty." The book continued to tell why she became a paleontologist despite the fact that some people thought that was a job for men. That sparked a great discussion.

In our email to Cathy, I relayed the children's request to see Cathy's toy "Bronty," which she did bring to the interview. The children already knew Cathy and Jim's stories from the books and the videos we used for our research, so the starting point for the questions at the interview was at quite a high level. Each question answered brought on another question, from children and their families. We had invited some children from other classes in our school—kids whose teachers thought they were passionate about paleontology. Touching a real tailbone from a dinosaur was a great thrill. Everyone just had to know if Jim was the man in Matthew's poem, the guy who found the Velociraptor bones in the Gobi Desert, the guy in the book, and the video. Indeed he was! What a thrill. The kids decided that we had to paint Jim's beard into our mural.

These twenty-nine first graders plus guests asked questions for nearly two hours without letup. There was almost no wiggling and no fooling around the whole time. I would never have forced young children to sit that long. That would have been inappropriate. But, when children keep raising their hands with more questions, when their eyes still have that sparkle, *you don't stop*. That's why we need schools where a subject is not restricted to a single forty-five-minute period, or where you stop when the bell rings. We need *time*, we need the right to go with the flow, time to follow the children's interests. In *Lifetime Guarantees, Toward Ambitious Literacy Teaching*, Shelley Harwayne talks about the need to have big blocks of time.

At last, we ended the double interview and moved to our "paleontologically correct" luncheon, prepared by the families. Oh, there was shell pasta salad, dino nuggets, fossil and dinosaur cookies, and so much more—a real feast. Then we presented a check from the families for $225.00 to help build a second school for the children in Madagascar. While Cathy's group had worked in Madagascar, they found that the children in the area had no school. The first school was so popular that they agreed to sponsor another school.

So many family members had taken off from work, came during their lunch hours, or brought their babies to this delightful interview/luncheon. Even James' grandfather, Morris, was there for this special interview.

Extending Beyond the Interview

This interview was a culmination of our research about paleontologists. It happened so late in the year, we didn't even have time to write a homemade book. All of our work in the various curriculum areas came before the interview.

What Did This Interview Have to Do with Behavior and Values?

CARRYING OUT SOCIAL ACTION

Cathy had helped start a school in Madagascar. Telling us about the school and the continued efforts to fund and expand the school was an inspiration. The paleontologists had taken action to improve the lives of children in Madagascar. We felt great that we helped in that effort.

SERVING AS ROLE MODELS

Both Cathy and Jim were so enthusiastic about their work. A parent asked them at the interview why they chose to be paleontologists. Cathy replied that she totally loves her work. *That is so important for the children to see.*

STAYING FOCUSED

This was a long interview, one that was filled with a variety of activities: questions and answers, role-plays, note taking, slides, touching a real dinosaur bone, and so on. The children had learned to stay focused, when there was some variety within the interview, and of course, when the interview was interesting.

Interview—Ione Batista, Matthew's mother

Matthew's mother, Ione, worked with her husband as a building superintendent. Ione and I talked in the school yard about Matthew's progress in school and about her family. Early in the year, when Ione told me she was from Brazil, I tucked that information inside. The last two months of the year, when we were planning our research about child labor, I knew we should interview Ione because there is a tremendous amount of child labor in Brazil.

At the interview, Matthew sat next to his mother, as is our custom. Both Ione and Matthew told us about child labor in Brazil—about children who pick coffee beans, take care of other people's homes, chop rocks, work as cowboys, sell newspapers and candy in the streets, and work in markets. Ione told us about families who live under the bridges and drink and bathe in the rivers.

Expanding Beyond the Interview

This interview became so important in the development of skills in the different curriculum areas.

DIRECTED WRITING AND ART

At the interview, the children took notes in their interview journals. By this time in the year, the children had stopped taking notes with pictures. Some took notes when I stopped and directed them to. Others were taking running notes throughout the interview. This is an important skill.

Then the children each wrote and illustrated a page for the homemade book about Ione. Doing this kind of directed writing week after week resulted in great improvement in every child's writing. The children learned how to focus on their page, how to develop concepts, how to edit and revise, as well as other skills. There is a kind of discipline in this type of directed writing.

READING

We did word study with the book about Ione, and then the children read and discussed the homemade book with their families as part of the homework.

WRITING

At Writing Workshop, numerous children wrote poems about child labor in Brazil and about child labor in general. It gave me great pleasure on the last day of school to hear James say, "My favorite thing was poetry. At first I thought poetry was boring. Then I saw that it wasn't." James, Matthew, and a whole group of children became really serious poets. They wrote really wonderful poems that they housed in small, blank, hardcover books. Also, they copied a number of their poems about child labor on large paper and posted them on a bulletin board for all to see. It was thrilling to see the depth of these children's enthusiasm. I believe this was due in part to how interesting our interview was and to the accessibility of the information.

ART AND WRITING

At Center Time for several days, a group of children worked with me to make a mural about the child cowboys. Children wrote labels to accompany the mural. The mural became the scenery in part of the play we wrote.

What Did This Interview Have to Do with Behavior and Values?

BUILDING SELF-ESTEEM

Matthew was bursting with pride that his mother was teaching his friends so much about their country.

HAVING A POTENTIAL IMPACT ON THE WHOLE FAMILY

I found out that Ione had been a teacher in Brazil. When she moved here, she helped her husband who became a superintendent. I have since encouraged Ione to prepare to go back to teaching after her younger son, Alex, enters kindergarten in the fall. That close involvement in our classroom was so important to Ione's life and the lives of her whole family.

WRITING AND BUILDING SELF-ESTEEM THROUGH A COMMUNITY EFFORT

When we sat down in early May to write a play about child labor, the children remembered what Ione had told them about child labor in Brazil. In a straw poll, the children voted unanimously to make one scene about the children who picked coffee beans in Brazil. In the final script of the play, the children say,

> "Did *you* know that children pick the beans for *your* coffee? Matthew's mother Ione told us about that. She's from Brazil." After a few "abracadabras," they go to Brazil, where the audience sees children picking coffee beans with their families.

Can you imagine how it felt to Matthew to have the information from his mother become a centerpiece for a class play, a play they performed at the Family Celebration in front of more than 125 family members and friends and then in front of their peers! Imagine what it did for the children who did the research, wrote, and then performed their play. We had done meaningful social action and we had built a strong, supportive, cooperative classroom community.

In Summary

These were just a few of our interviews. You can see from this brief outline that the interviews helped the children develop skills in so many curriculum areas. Also, so important is that the interviews helped shape the children's values and behavior.

8

Literature Can Help Develop Values

In Chapter 1 of this book, I talked about the kind of classroom community I want to develop. It is important to me that the children be honest, caring, kind, cooperative, and supportive to each other and to adults. If you're looking for role models for such wholesome values, literature is a wonderful source. The characters are just waiting to tell their stories. They're just calling out to get you to think or to examine your own life. Sometimes it's easier to have children look at themselves through characters in literature than it is to have them do this through a direct approach.

In addition to developing values, literature can help our students deal with problems. Our students may face problems that are difficult for some teachers to imagine: homelessness, family members in jail, unemployment, parents who are not home, violence, abuse, separation and divorce, mental health problems, frequent moving, poor or no supervision, death or dying, neglect even by parents who are present, and so on. Or the problems could be related to the birth of a sibling or sibling rivalry. Then there are the many school-related problems such as friendships, isolation, competition, meanness, and so on. Any of these or other problems can impact on a child's learning and behavior in the classroom or at recess and lunch, which are usually less supervised times.

Looking at an issue through literature can help an individual child or children in a class look at how the characters in the story cope with or solve problems. It may help children find strategies for dealing with difficult problems. For example, sometimes I select a book because it deals with a problem faced by children in the class. I may read or lend a book to a single child. Or I may have a read aloud with the whole class. Of course, you need to be extremely sensitive about this. There are certain problems and issues that must be kept private (among the child, family, and teacher).

Usually, I read a book without discussing my intention. Children may see themselves in the characters (people or animals) of the book. But, in a whole class discussion, they may choose to speak about their own issues or problems or to remain silent. The purpose of the read aloud is definitely *not* to embarrass a child by placing her in the spotlight or by exposing her problem. It is also not an indictment of a child or family. In a whole class discussion that child may find out that other children face a similar problem. You may be able to help those children find time to talk together during the day or after school. Sometimes friendships evolve because of a common problem. It is often such a great relief to a child when he knows that the teacher and the other children know that he is hurting inside because of this kind of problem. Sometimes that relief actually turns into much improved behavior. The support evolving from the discussions after these read alouds can be invaluable.

Fiction Versus Nonfiction

I'm not fond of nonfiction books that merely describe the meaning and the issues of divorce, death and dying, different values, and so on. While these books have lots of facts and information, they may not be the right books for your read alouds. Many are poorly written. In fact, while I often use nonfiction for our research in science or social studies, I rarely use nonfiction to deal with these kinds of personal issues or with values.

I prefer reading quality fiction or historical fiction, whether it's folktales, fairytales, or just stories. Fiction brings out the sentiments, the feelings, and the humanity. We can see ourselves by looking at the problems and issues of others, be they animals, people, or even fantasy characters. The bibliography includes a list of books that are mentioned here as well as other related fiction literature. The list is multicultural in essence so that children will see literature from and by authors from different races, cultures, and countries.

Where to Find Appropriate Books

When I want to develop a particular value, or when I want to help children deal with problems, I think right away about what literature could support this effort. First, I comb through my classroom and my home libraries. Then I ask colleagues, friends, workers at bookstores, or librarians. Often I'll put a note in the Family Homework to ask the family members for help. A new tool for finding appropriate books is to look at the online bookstores. When you look at the title of a book with a particular issue such as friendship, the company will suggest titles with a similar theme.

Always Preview Books

I have a very important rule for myself. I *always preview a book* before I decide whether to read it to my class. Someone else's favorite book may not work for your class. Taste in books is very personal. The book may not be age-appropriate. Perhaps it doesn't deal with the issue the way you had hoped. It just might not be the kind of writing you care for.

Literature to Encourage Positive Behaviors

Dealing with Meanness

Sometimes we can use literature to help children examine their own negative behavior or the behavior of characters in literature or to help provide an example of positive behavior. For example, there was some nasty, sharp-edged talk by one of the girls toward another girl in our class. I knew from talking with the kindergarten teacher that this was an ongoing problem. I spoke to the child about an incident that day, and she apologized to the child she had offended. At Meeting that day, I chose to read one of my favorite books, *Mufaro's Beautiful Daughters: An African Tale*, by John Steptoe. The folktale is about two sisters, Nyasha, a kind and considerate girl, and Manyara, a selfish, bad-tempered, jealous, and spoiled girl. Nyasha is kind to her father, helps the old woman, gives food to the little boy, and is kind to the garden snake (who eventually becomes the king and her husband). I read with lots of expression, making Nyasha's voice very gentle and Manyara's very harsh. The class just loved Nyasha. They were clearly upset by Manyara. During the book talk, they talked about what made them like Nyasha and dislike Manyara. Looking at the children, I could see that some recognized these types of characters in themselves or in others in the class, although we didn't name names. Later in the day, I quietly talked with the child who had been harsh and asked her why she thought I read that book. She knew that the book was for her. I encouraged her to work hard on this problem. And she did.

The folktale *The Talking Eggs: A Folktale from the American South*, by Robert D. San Souci, based in Louisiana, has a similar theme. I used this book when there was just too much meanness coming from a small group of children in the class. In this story, there is a good daughter, Blanche, and a mean daughter, Rose. You should have heard my voice as I read the words of the two daughters. I used such a gentle and soft voice for Blanche, and a mean and snippy voice for Rose. I really exaggerated their voices, and I knew very well that the culprits in our classroom heard themselves in my voice, though I said nothing. As we discussed the story in groups of two or three and then with the whole class, children talked about how they loved the good daughter and disliked the mean daughter. We talked about what kinds of things Blanche did that made her such a wonderful person. A child raised his hand to speak, "That sounds just like in the story about the two daughters and the king." Another child reminded him of the title, *Mufaro's Beautiful Daughters*. Still another child said that reminded him of Martin Luther King. One after the other children remembered characters from other stories we had read, wonderful people we had interviewed, or people we had learned about during the year. For some it reminded them of wonderful people in their own lives. Of course, I was delighted. These characters would serve as role models during the year and perhaps for a lifetime.

Because there were several children in our class involved in the meanness, I wanted to have the whole class see the relevance of the book to our own lives. Then I asked if anyone knew why I had chosen this story. Some of the culprits looked downwards to avoid being called on. One brave soul (one of the culprits) said that it was probably because of the way they had acted earlier in the day. "Yup," I nodded and said, "and some of you sounded a little like Blanche and her mother." A full and deep discussion ensued.

For children who love animals, Eric Carle's *The Grouchy Ladybug* is just terrific. The grouchy ladybug fights with the good ladybug about who will get to eat the aphids on the leaves. The good ladybug is willing to share, but the grouchy ladybug just wants to fight. The grouchy ladybug challenges other animals, from the flea to the great whale, to no avail. In the end, the ladybugs agree to share the aphids.

Dealing with Greed, Vanity, Spoiled Behavior, and Showing Off

We laughed our way through *The Girl Who Wore Too Much: A Folktale from Thailand*, by S. Vathanaprida, illustrated by Y. L. Davis. This story is about a girl who is vain and wants to show off her fancy clothing, so she puts on more and more clothes, one on top of the other, until she can't even get up the hill to join the other children at a dance. In our classroom community, I try to play down the issue of clothing, shoes, and jewelry. In our class, showing off is not a virtue. Acting superior to others is unacceptable. This delightful book, with great illustrations and writing in both English and Thai, brought that point home.

In *How Mr. Monkey Saw the Whole World*, by Walter Dean Myers, illustrated by Synthia Saint James, the buzzard was so selfish and mean. We roared with laughter as buzzard took the other animals high in the sky and demanded food to keep him from dropping them. Well, he learned his lesson and had to return the food.

This story reminded the children of the lazy and greedy Anansi, in *Anansi and the Moss-Covered Rock*, retold by Eric Kimmel, illustrated by Janet Stevens. Anansi

126

stories originated from the Ashanti people in Ghana and have traveled all over the world. Anansi, whether he is a spider, a man, or takes some other form, is always up to no good. He takes things from others who are doing the work. He likes to get something for nothing. He's a regular trickster who makes us laugh as we watch him make mischief. And we learn our lessons about morality in the process.

There are many versions of the old folktale, *King Midas and the Golden Touch*, which deals with the theme of greed. During our read aloud, the children had a strong reaction when the King's daughter, who is probably around their age, was about to be turned into gold. They were calling out, "No, no, don't touch her!" Oh, that led to a great discussion about how greedy that king was. We talked also about the issue of having material goods as opposed to friendship and love.

In *Berlioz the Bear*, by Jan Brett, each animal boasted that he could get the mule out of the hole so the musicians would be able to go to the gala ball. The larger the animal, the more it boasted. The children noticed the pattern with the animals getting smaller and smaller. None of that bravado of the animals who were boasting so much paid off because it was the tiny bee that stung the mule and made him jump to his feet and pull the bandwagon, which got to the ball just on time. The children were delighted by that small bee.

Catherine Stock wrote *Where Are You Going Manyoni?*—the perfect book for children who are not satisfied with all of their material goods or the things that are done for them. Manyoni gets up early and walks alone through the countryside of Zimbabwe to get to the school she loves so much. She watches the bushpig and the impala feeding as she walks. Manyoni has none of the material goods that some of our students may have, yet she experiences the joys of life and learning without complaint.

The main character in Taro Yashima's *Crow Boy* walks a long distance through the mountains to get to school. He is not like the other children. Also, he is a very modest child. Others in his class laugh at his simplicity until they see that he can imitate the many different calls of the crows. Finally, they see that he is an extraordinary person.

Dealing with Dishonesty

The innkeeper in the Norse folktale, *Peter and the North Wind*, retold by Freya Littledale, illustrated by Troy Howell, was a dishonest man. He kept stealing things from Peter. As I read this story from Norway, children remarked that the innkeeper was just like Bumba, in *Akimba and the Magic Cow: A Folktale from Africa*, retold by Anne Rose, illustrated by Hope Meryman. I asked the children how we could have an almost identical story from two different parts of the world. We looked at the map to see how far apart they were. Children had all sorts of guesses: someone took them there by boat or airplane, someone heard them on the radio or TV, and so on. We talked about the fact that these were old stories that may have been here long before planes, radios, or TV. Yes, these stories could have come with people who traveled or were taken to other countries (such as stories of African peoples who were taken by force to the Americas). We thought about the notion that every country probably has some people who are honest or dishonest, so people everywhere probably make up their own stories about that. We talked about how people all over the world make up or tell stories to teach the children right from wrong. The style of storytelling in these folktales helps you laugh as you examine the issues.

I mention Anansi stories in several parts of this chapter. I love how his mischievous character just scoops the children up into a fantasy world and leads them to take a closer look at human behavior. Anansi is often lazy and greedy, and quite dishonest. Anansi stories help children see that Anansi's dishonesty hurts the other characters. Anansi never looks good in the end, and his dishonesty never ever pays off. (Anansi's name is spelled in a few different ways.)

In the old Chinese folktale, *The Empty Pot*, by Demi, the Emperor was looking for a successor. He gave flower seeds to all of the children, but he would let the flowers choose the child who was the best in a year's time. After a year's time, the children brought their beautiful flowering plants to show the Emperor, but Ping still had an empty pot. He had tried in vain to make the seed grow. The Emperor rewarded Ping for his honesty. The children didn't know that the seeds had all been cooked, and cooked seeds can't grow! It is a touching story with very lovely art work. My students really loved Ping. They requested that we reread the story a few times. Rereading is a real treat. You can often see so much more in a story or in illustrations the second time.

Learning to Follow the Rules

If you read *Tortoise's Dream*, by Joanna Troughton, with expression, your class will roll with laughter as the animals of the forest boast and then fail, one after the other, to follow the rules. When Tortoise follows the rules, down come the bananas, the dates, the coconuts, the melons, and more from the Omumborombonga tree. Tortoise shares the seeds of these fruits with the animals who plant them all over. It's so funny to hear children (sometimes even the mischief makers) laugh and talk about this story.

Dealing with Sharing

In *Ananse's Feast: An Ashanti Tale*, retold by Tololwa M. Mollel, illustrated by Andrew Glass, Ananse doesn't want to share his food with Turtle during the drought. He does all sorts of ridiculous things to avoid sharing, but Turtle teaches him a lesson, until the next time. When Ananse carries on like this, it enables children to look within themselves. We all laugh to think of Ananse doing so much to avoid sharing.

Combating Prejudice, Stereotyping, and Discrimination

There are several books that are in the category of historical fiction or nonfiction that help us examine the issues of prejudice, stereotyping, and discrimination. *Teammates*, by Peter Golenbrock, illustrated by Paul Bacon, is about Jackie Robinson's life. We meet Branch Rickey, the general manager of the Brooklyn Dodgers, who asked Jackie to join the team, despite the strong opposition to having someone Black on the team. Then, we meet Pee Wee Reese, a teammate who spoke up and defended Jackie's right to be on the team. Over the years several of my classes have turned this story into a play and performed it for their families and for other classes in the school. The bravery of Jackie and the boldness of Pee Wee stay deep in the hearts and minds of so many of the children.

The first time I read *Nobody Owns the Sky: The Story of "Brave Bessie" Coleman*, by Reeve Lindbergh, illustrated by Pamela Paparone, I was stunned by this lyrical poem about a courageous struggle against discrimination. What a delightful way to tell such an important story. Bessie Coleman faced discrimination all her life. She met a lot of resistance when she decided to become a pilot, not only because she was African American, but because she was a woman. None of the aviation schools in the United States would accept her, so Bessie studied in France. She became the first African American woman pilot.

Right away in the discussion children remembered other stories we had read about overcoming discrimination. They recalled stories such as *Alvin Ailey*, by Andrea Davis Pinkney, illustrated by Brian Pinkney, where Alvin Ailey was turned away from dance schools because he was African American. Not only did he achieve his dream, but he established a dance company and school to provide opportunity to other people of color. What a fine role model.

Another important book is *The Story of Ruby Bridges*, by Robert Coles, illustrated by George Ford. This is the story of a six-year-old African American girl who, in 1960, was ordered by a judge to go to an all-white elementary school. It's a story of courage in the midst of hateful discrimination. *Happy Birthday, Martin Luther King*, by Jean Marzollo, illustrated by J. Brian Pinkney, tells the story of Martin Luther King, Jr.'s life and his efforts to help end segregation. Brian Pinkney's scratch art is breathtaking. A *Picture Book of Jesse Owens*, by David A. Adler, illustrated by Robert Casilla, begins with Jesse's life as the son of sharecroppers in Alabama. It goes on to tell of those who supported Jesse in becoming a fine athlete, and eventually an Olympic champion. As a hero in the 1936

129

Olympics in Germany, he was scorned by Hitler. It was interesting to see how many children had heard of Hitler in discussions at home and how many had great-grandparents who fought in World War II. Even on his return to the United States, he faced discrimination. Over the years, each of these books has inspired murals, stories at Writing Workshop, and even class plays.

The fictional book, *Amazing Grace*, by Mary Hoffman, illustrated by Caroline Binch, is a lovely story about Grace, who wanted to be Peter Pan in her class play. One child whispered "No," because Grace was a girl. Another said, "No," because Grace was Black. Encouraged by her grandmother, who took her to see a friend from Trinidad dancing as Juliet, in *Romeo and Juliet*, Grace practiced hard for the audition. Her classmates agreed that she was the best, and so Grace was selected to be Peter Pan in the play. Some of the children burst into Langston Hughes' poem, *Dreams*, in the middle of the book talk. This book is especially useful because Grace is a young girl fighting against discrimination.

Building Community—Working Together

For a fabulous way to get children to talk about working together, read *Swimmy* by Leo Lionni, which is about small fish that are being gobbled up by the big tuna fish. Swimmy suggests that all of the small fish get together to form one large fish so the tuna will not eat them. This book was great for talking about unions during our study of People at Work.

It Takes a Village, by Jane Cowen-Fletcher is about a young boy, Yemi, who wanders away from his sister who is watching him while their mother sells mangoes at a market in Benin, West Africa. The mother and sister aren't worried because they know that people at the market will take care of Yemi. This is a wonderful look at a community working together.

When we have a read aloud with Lynne Cherry's book, *A River Ran Wild*, the children are entranced. It's a fabulous book about the efforts of people to clean up the Nashua River that flows through Massachusetts and New Hampshire. The Native people named the river, Nash-a-way River with the Pebbled Bottom. Over time the settlers built factories, which spewed dyes and other chemicals into the river. People joined together to fight for legislation to protect the river from dumping. Once again, the pebbles shine up through clear water. Of course, the children ask right away if this is a true story. While it is based on a true story, there are a few elements that seem like fiction. This story is a great introduction to the concept of historical fiction. In fact, both the front and the back of the book have details about the efforts to clean the river and provide a greenway along its banks.

Friendship, Love, and Taking Care of Others

In *Uncle Willie and the Soup Kitchen*, by DyAnne DiSalvo-Ryan, Uncle Willie takes his nephew to a soup kitchen where he volunteers. The nephew, who tells the story, not only gets to see what happens at the soup kitchen, but he sees the humanity of the other workers and people who eat there. This book has inspired many of my classes to collect food for a soup kitchen.

Something from Nothing, by Phoebe Gilman, was adapted from a Jewish folktale. When Joseph is born, his grandfather makes him a wonderful blue blanket. The blanket gets worn out, so the grandfather turns the blanket into a jacket. When the jacket no longer fits, the grandfather says, "Hmm, as his scissors went snip, snip, snip and his needle flew in and out in and out." When you read this book, the children are drawn into the story as the blue cloth gets smaller and smaller. After only a few pages, they, too, are saying, "Hmm, as his scissors went snip, snip, snip . . ." until the end of the story when the button the grandfather made from the blue cloth gets lost. Since the grandfather couldn't make something from nothing, Joseph used his pen to write a story about the blue cloth. The book talk can be very moving, as children in the class feel the love and caring in the story.

It's so important that children see characters in literature who love and care for each other. *A Pocket for Corduroy*, by Don Freeman, is a simple story of a girl and her toy bear named Corduroy who gets left at the laundromat. Corduroy tells Lisa that he wandered away because he was looking for a pocket. The next morning, Lisa affectionately sews a pocket on Corduroy's overalls.

The Wednesday Surprise, by Eve Bunting, illustrated by Donald Carrick, is a lovely story about a young girl named Anna who teaches her grandmother to read. The grandmother reads to Anna's father for his birthday. This book gets the children thinking about helping others.

Molly Bang's book, *The Paper Crane*, is a beautiful story about a restaurant owner who feeds a stranger who is unable to pay. Because a new highway had been built, the restaurant was no longer on the main road, and there were no more customers. In return for the kindness of the owner, the stranger folds a napkin into a paper crane. This mysterious bird attracts many customers to the restaurant. Children love this story and see such a great example of kindness and of people helping each other.

Vera B. Williams has a series of three stories, *A Chair for My Mother*, *Something Special for Me*, and *Music, Music for Everyone*, which are so useful in dealing with a number of issues. The family in the three books is a single parent family, a mother, daughter, and grandmother. In *Music, Music for Everyone*, the grandmother gets sick, and the child and her friends pitch in to help out. In *A Chair for My Mother*, the neighbors and relatives help them deal with a fire which destroyed their apartment. I read this book after 9/11 so that children could see that it is often ordinary people, relatives and neighbors, who help each other during a crisis.

In *Anansi the Spider: A Tale from the Ashanti*, by Gerald McDermott, Father Anansi gets into trouble. His six sons come to his rescue. Each helps the father in a different way, but it is the son, Cushion, who cushions the blow when Anansi falls from the sky. Nyami, the God of All Things wonders who should get the prize for rescuing Anansi. Nyami can't decide and so puts the prize, the great ball of light, into the sky for all to see. This story is not funny like most Anansi tales, but it enables us to raise important issues with our students, the issues of cooperation and taking care of others. I read this story to my class shortly after the tragedy at the World Trade Center where the media focused on the rescue efforts of the police and fire departments. In fact, there were many others who helped in so many ways—other workers from the buildings and people from the surrounding community. There were people who donated blood, who provided food for rescue workers, who counseled people, and so on. We interviewed Allison Snyder's father, Robert, a teacher and journalist who documented the rescue efforts of maritime workers on 9/11.

After reading *Anansi the Spider: A Tale from the Ashanti* and *A Chair for My Mother* our class painted a four-part mural about the issue of cooperation. The first panel was people helping at the World Trade Center, the second was a scene from *Anansi the Spider*, the third was a page from *A Chair for My Mother*, and the last was a painting of the tug boats and Staten Island Ferry and the maritime workers we learned about from Allison's father.

There are poems that come to mind when I think about friendship. One is "Poem," by Langston Hughes, about a friend that went away. It can be found in *The Dream Keeper and Other Poems*, by Langston Hughes, illustrated by Brian Pinkney. Another, "If I Had a Paka," is a poem written in Swahili and English and can be found in the book *If I Had a Paka: Poems in Eleven Languages*, by Charlotte Pomerantz, illustrated by Nancy Tafuri.

Literature to Help Deal with Life's Problems

Dealing with Health Problems or Accidents

Many children have parents, siblings, or other relatives who are sick or have suffered from strokes, accidents, or other serious health problems. Tomie dePaola's *Now One Foot, Now the Other*, is a touching story about a grandfather who helps his grandson to walk, now one foot, now the other. When the grandfather has a stroke and gradually gets back his ability to feed himself, to recognize his loved ones, to smile, his grandson teaches him to walk, now one foot, now the other. I can hardly read it without tears welling in my eyes.

Overcoming Problems or Dealing with Many Problems

Uncle Jed's Barbershop, by Margaree King Mitchell, is a marvelous book for dealing with a number of issues. Uncle Jed tried to fulfill his dream of opening his own barber shop. He lived in the deep South around the time of the Great Depression. Uncle Jed faced discrimination because he was Black. He saved his money. My students were struck by how thoughtful Uncle Jed was when he used his savings to help pay for his niece's operation. He saved again. Then, he lost his savings during the Depression when the banks closed. At age 79, he finally opened his barber shop. This a great book for thinking about persevering despite all of the obstacles that may be in our way.

Dealing with Disabilities

Wilma Unlimited: How Wilma Rudolph Became the World's Fastest Woman, by Kathleen Krull, tells the story of Wilma Rudolph. Wilma, a very sickly child, grew up in the deep South. When she contracted polio, she had to travel with her mother fifty miles by bus to the nearest hospital that would treat a Black person. Wilma was excluded from school because she was wearing a brace on her leg. Wilma was determined to walk without the brace and to walk. Not only did Wilma fulfill her dream to walk and go to school, but she won four gold medals in track and field at the 1960 Olympics. She later established an organization to help young people get an education and to become athletes.

Dealing with a Parent in Prison

Vera B. Williams' book, *Amber Was Brave, Essie Was Smart: The Story of Amber and Essie Told Here in Poems and Pictures*, deals with a family who lives in poverty as well as a father who is released from prison. A number of times I have had children in my class who had mothers or fathers in prison. This information was always confidential so we never had read alouds about this topic those years. This is a book I might choose to give to a parent or to read to a class of older children that didn't have a student with a parent in prison.

In Summary

Literature can open doors to some of the most difficult topics. The characters in the stories enable children to examine negative behavior and to see positive role models. It is a wonderful tool for developing values. Using literature to help children learn to be decent to each other and to work together can bring about improved behavior in the classroom and in the world.

Some may say young children shouldn't be exposed to literature that deals with life's problems. To ignore such problems is to ignore the reality of children's family life. Just ask, and you'll hear about relatives who use walkers, canes, hearing aids, and more. Many families' lives are complicated by the care of ill family members or relatives or by problems such as having a relative in prison. Talking about it openly (either privately with the child or with the whole class) is often a great relief to a child. That relief can translate into improved behavior and greater focus on schoolwork.

9

Working with Special
Needs Children

The Story of a Child We Will Call Sibby*

When Sibby was in the kindergarten class, I watched her teacher, my friend Bella, welcome Sibby and help her navigate becoming part of their classroom community. We talked about Sibby constantly. It was a wonder watching Sibby, a child with Down Syndrome, who entered school with an additional problem—she was unable to say most consonants. Can you imagine not being able to use consonants? How would you communicate? Try to say, "I love you," without using consonants. Ask your friends some questions without using consonants. Can they understand you? Can you imagine being the teacher of twenty-eight children, one of whom is unable to use consonants?

That's inclusion in New York City—taking in and welcoming a special needs child or children into your classroom community. Is it easy? *No*, not even for an experienced teacher. It's not easy for the special needs child, the other children, the teacher, and the families. However, if you have a positive attitude about inclusion, if you really believe in inclusion, if your school believes in inclusion and provides adequate support services, and if you work closely with the families, it can work. Not always. But, beginning with a positive attitude and constantly searching for ways to make it work, can result in success. Having a smaller class would certainly help.

Bella believed in inclusion. Sibby came to class with what we call in our school district a management paraprofessional. That was essential because there were times when Sibby needed extra help with regular kindergarten activities, as well as getting up and down stairs, getting her coat off and so on. Sibby was stubborn, oh so stubborn, as is common with many Down Syndrome children. In

---

*The names of the child, parents, and paraprofessionals are fictious. The story is real.

addition, she had very few tools for communication—so when she couldn't be understood or couldn't get her way, screaming, stamping her feet, and fussing were her tools. Bella had to help Sibby communicate more effectively. The speech teacher, Tina, was truly wonderful. She helped Bella, and later me, understand that we had to help Sibby train her brain to send messages to her lips and tongue to make the proper movements to pronounce consonants. By the end of kindergarten, Sibby could say a few consonants.

Also, Bella and the paraprofessional had to help Sibby conform to the structures and the routines in the classroom—not an easy task. Bella and I agreed that you had to be very strict, very consistent, very loving, and very funny in order to succeed with Sibby. You had to involve the whole class in the effort. When Bella asked me if I would be Sibby's teacher in first grade, I was so honored and so excited. I had worked with many special needs children in my early years who had not yet been evaluated. That was mainstreaming of the worst sort, because the classes were large—there were sometimes as many as eight children with very serious problems in a classroom—and, in those years, there was absolutely *no* support. Most of those special needs children ended up in self-contained special education classes after first grade.

Sibby's parents, two very aware and wonderful people, had her evaluation completed very early, so she entered kindergarten already eligible for a management paraprofessional, speech and language, and other services. These services would be continued in the first grade. Here was a new experience for me, a special needs child and nearly every kind of support available.

When she entered our class, Sibby was clumsy, stubborn, very funny, not completely toilet trained, loving, and immature. Her play with other children resembled parallel play. She loved music so much that when the music teacher or I played music and sang with the class each day, her whole body burst into life and swung to the music. Eva, Sibby's new maintenance paraprofessional, is a musician. Eva really enjoyed Sibby's love of music.

Creating Community

What did we do to help bring Sibby into a community where building friends was just as important as developing academic skills?

- I met with Bella and Sibby's parents while Sibby was still in kindergarten. I wanted Sandy and John to be comfortable with me, and I wanted to get to know them and learn more about Sibby.
- Bella sent Sibby to my class with a support group, children who had been very supportive to Sibby in kindergarten. That was so important. They were already aware of Sibby's issues, and they were so supportive of Sibby.

- We welcomed Sibby into our class. When she was out of the room to receive special services, I took time to talk with the other children openly about Sibby so they would have some understanding of her situation and the role I wanted them to play.

- Some children treated Sibby in what might be called a patronizing way—almost like a doll. They did so out of love and caring. It was not at all malicious. They had to learn how to play and work with Sibby as a real person. For example, they would often help Sibby get up. I had to tell them to let Sibby get up by herself—not so easy, but she could do it.

- The children were extremely helpful teaching Sibby how to say the sounds of the consonants. I often modeled that. I would say, "Sibby, watch my lips." I would say a word or a phrase. "Now, Sibby, you say it." She worked so hard. So often, you would see the other children do the same. Sibby would repeat their words. This was essential because it was that constant work with the speech teacher and the repetition in the class and at home that enabled Sibby to speak and be understood better by the last few months of her first year with me and Eva.

- When I met with the families on Curriculum Night, I spoke openly about Sibby and her needs and the role I wanted the children and them to play. The families told me often that they were delighted to see the powerful impact of this experience on their children and on themselves.

- Sibby was extraordinarily stubborn. Rather than be angry with her, I tried to understand the many reasons for that behavior beyond the fact that many Down Syndrome children can be quite stubborn. I knew that she could barely be understood. Wouldn't that be a good reason to be stubborn? I spoke at length with Bella and with people who knew about Down Syndrome. I spoke with the speech teachers. We were going to find any way possible to turn around the stubborn behavior. Here are some of the things we did.

Set limits: explain the consequences for inappropriate behavior. I told Sibby that she should could not scream, stamp her feet, refuse to sit down, or whatever inappropriate behavior she was caught up in at the moment. I told her the consequence. "Sibby, if you scream, and you don't sit down now, you will have time-out at Center Time. Sibby loved Center Time, so that often worked. She would scream and cry. Then she would say in her difficult-to-understand way, "I ah-ee. I eher oo i aen." (I'm sorry. I'll never do it again.) No matter how many times she apologized, I insisted that she have that short time-out. She would cry again, just to think about having time-out. At Center Time, Sibby sat for a few minutes of time out without a whimper. Then she hurried to play. That was difficult for us to bear, with all of her crying and fussing, but I was pretty sure that this would work. It did.

Explain the rules regarding classroom behaviors and the consequence. One day Eva was at lunch. We were having Writing Workshop. I was juggling working with Sibby and several other children. When Sibby finished her picture, I asked her to put the marker down and pick up a pencil because I was going to help her with the writing. I reminded her that in our class we use pencils for writing. She refused and fussed. I warned her that I might seem mean. I told Sibby that I would not help her until she put down her marker and picked up her pencil. Again, I explained why. I told her that I would just help the other children, and that when she wanted to follow the rules, I would help her. She screamed and cried and fussed. Children could hardly concentrate on their writing. I was being strict, not mean. A little while later Sibby said to me, "au-a, I eh-y ow." (Paula, I'm ready now.) We sat together and worked, Sibby, with pencil in hand. The next day, Sibby drew her picture, and then picked up a pencil when she was ready for help with the writing. From that moment on, Sibby followed that rule, and she was able to move smoothly from drawing to writing.

Sibby had to learn certain positive behaviors. I strongly believed that she was capable of that. I had to be strict and unyielding in this effort if Sibby would continue to be mainstreamed in school and to live a full and productive life, as we all believed she could.

LAUGH

I had to laugh with Sibby. I love laughter, so this one came naturally to me. Sibby would fuss and carry on. It seemed like there would be no way to get her to sit down and join us at story circle, reading, or other activities. I knew that one important way to reach Sibby (and most children) was through humor. I might look angrily at Sibby and say, "Sibby, if you don't sit down right now . . . I'm gonna send you to the moon." Sibby would go from fussing, to laughing. Once the tension was broken, she would sit down and participate. Often, especially early in the first year, we had to use humor to get through to Sibby. Her smile and her laugh were gigantic. The whole class enjoyed her laughter and came to love it when it got Sibby through those very frequent rough spots.

LOVE

Love, not pity, was an important ingredient. Being Sibby's teacher was a challenge. I loved her so much. Her love of music, of laughter, of other children, of life, was really endearing. Over the years I have had many children whose negative behaviors made it difficult to love them. I feel that it is my responsibility as a teacher to find something, anything, in a child, or to try to turn a child's behavior around so that I could love or at least like a child.

Sibby quickly grew to know that Eva and I loved her and that the class loved her. She knew I was strict, and she came to see that she could have a great time in class if she followed the rules. Little by little, we saw her behavior change. By having so many role models in our class, she learned about appropriate behaviors, something that is much more difficult to accomplish when a child is in a special education class where there might be a lot of inappropriate behavior.

COMMUNICATE WITH FAMILIES

We had a notebook that went back and forth between home and school. When we used the notebook, we wrote about both positive and negative things that happened in a day. I called Sandy at home or talked with John when he brought Sibby to school. Once, I called Sandy, and deliberately interrupted her work, just to tell her about a breakthrough Sibby had made in reading. It is very important that contact with family include problems as well as positive feedback. It is not easy to be the parent of a special needs child, especially if everything you hear from the school is negative. *Find something positive to tell the family*.

PRAISE

Oh, Sibby loved to be praised. Her early responses to praise were exaggerated. She would bow and curtsy, and bat her eyes. She was quite charming. We did have to help her modify her response and make it more appropriate.

USE LITERATURE TO TEACH THE CHILDREN MORE ABOUT DISABILITIES

To teach about disabilities, I do not read nonfiction books about the topic. Those books are often quite dull and inappropriate for young children. What is so much better are storybooks in which a character has special needs. There are a few really great books that I have used—*How Smudge Came*, by Nan Gregory, illustrated by Ron Lightburn. It's about a girl who looks as if she has Down Syndrome. The girl ends up adopting a dog and befriending the people in a nursing home she cleans. When Sibby was out of the room one day, I read that story to my class. The children said, "She looks like Sibby." We had a great talk. Another useful book is called *My Friend Jacob*, by Lucille Clifton, illustrated by Thomas DiGrazia. In this book a child makes friends with another child who seems to be disabled. They have a beautiful friendship. These book talks deepen the children's understanding about disabilities.

Seeing Success

Sibby repeated first grade with Eva and me. She had no problem adjusting to the new class. As the year unfolded, Sibby's ability to speak with consonants and to be understood improved dramatically. I'm sure this was a factor that helped turn her behavior around. We saw significant changes. Sibby was bold. She tried to participate all along, but it was so difficult for her. Now, she was bold, but more successful. That success and the praise she got from all of us moved her forward.

Sibby was empowered to be in charge of her own behavior. Not only did Sibby's behavior improve dramatically, but she was finally able to focus much more on her academic work in class and at the resource room program. Her reading, writing, and math improved. She got really involved in our social studies research—a wonderful area for her because it didn't require her to be a fluent reader or writer. During research workshop, Sibby asked questions. She developed critical thinking skills and participated in the discussions. It was somewhat difficult for the children to understand some of what she said, several of us (including children) served as interpreters when necessary.

Sibby started participating actively in role-plays during interviews. She loved the role-plays. During the role-plays and discussions, you could see how perceptive and intelligent Sibby really was. Sibby loved read-alouds and started speaking more during the book talk. She started having more two-way conversations with other children. Her play became less parallel and more interactive. She started going on more playdates after school. Even Sibby's posture improved. It was as if that new pride in herself helped her stand with pride.

Twice a year our class had a Family Celebration in the evening. We shared our songs and poems, our research and our homemade plays with the families. We made special efforts to prepare her so that she could go on stage with the other children. By the end of her second year in our class, Sibby was able to focus on the preparations for the Family Celebration. Sibby's moment of triumph came when she recited a poem she wrote during our research about child labor. She said her poem alone in front of nearly 125 family members and friends! There were many tears. So many people had participated in that triumph.

Sibby went on to second grade the next year with a teacher who was really looking forward to having Sibby in her class (that is so important). She continued to receive the same kinds of special services. With love and lots of support and understanding, Sibby will shine.

Why Is the Topic of Inclusion in a Book About *Discipline?*

Inclusion happens—sometimes in a planned way as in the case of Sibby, sometimes by default. So often teachers find themselves with special needs children who have not been evaluated, who are waiting for placement in self-contained classes, or who are not yet receiving special services. This can be difficult and very frustrating.

Sometimes families refuse to have their child evaluated by the school or they have evaluations done privately and refuse to show the school any results. It is so difficult for many families to come to terms with the fact that their child has serious learning or emotional problems. No one *wants* to have their child suffer from any kind of problem. I can understand that. We must be patient and continue to find ways to work with the family to help them through this difficult situation. In the interim, the child is in your class and is not receiving extra support.

Tips for Working with Special Needs Children

These tips can be used in the classroom with or without extra support services.

- Make the child feel welcome in your class.
- Speak to the class when the child is out of the room to help the children understand the nature of the problem and how they can be supportive. This might involve a role-play and/or a discussion. If appropriate, have a nurse, a guidance counselor, or other resource person talk with the students, and/or read a story with a character who faces a similar problem. In some cases, as with a child in my class who was diagnosed with Type I Diabetes, those discussions took place with the child in the classroom.
- Don't be angry with the child. If you think the child needs special services, such as resource room or even a self-contained special education class, and the family does not agree to an evaluation, do not be angry with the child. Do everything possible to provide a quality education. You may decide to continue to press for an evaluation. Continue to keep anecdotal records. Invite the family to volunteer in the classroom or to come just to observe their child. That parent may come to value your opinion.

Do not assume that the child should be in a self-contained special education class or that the problems will always be so severe. Do not always rush to have an evaluation. Sometimes, I wait several months before asking for that evaluation. There are many reasons for this:

- Sometimes the situation in the class before you was not good—the child and teacher did not get along, the teacher and parents did not get along, a new or inexperienced teacher who could not adequately help the child, a teacher who was frequently absent, which destabilized the class, and so on.
- Sometimes the child was experiencing a crisis at home—a separation, a divorce, a death, fighting, abuse, a birth of a sibling, a sibling leaving home, the loss of a job, and so on.

- Sometimes the child is just immature and needs time.
- Sometimes the child is influenced in inappropriate ways by other children in or outside of school.
- Sometimes a child needs a more rigorous curriculum. The child may be bored silly and unable to stay focused.
- Sometimes a child needs a less rigorous or a less complex curriculum. The child may be confused and unable to stay focused.

Work Closely with the Family

Try to learn more about the child's family life, history, customs, economic situation (in the case of unemployment or multiple jobs), problems, talents, and so on. All of this will help you understand the child and will inform your teaching. For example, you may find out that there is no adult at home with the child in the evening or no one to help the child with schoolwork or problems. You may find out that there is a history of dyslexia, mental illness, or other chronic illnesses in the family. It's best to have these conversations in person, before or after school, in the evening if that is possible for you, or during lunch or a free period. Sometimes you may have to talk on the phone if the family is not available to come to the school.

- Invite the families to help in the classroom or school. While they are helping, you can get to know them and their family better. You can take time to talk about their child. You can show them ways to work with their child at home.
- Help the family navigate the system if they decide to have the child evaluated. Inform them of their rights in the process so they don't feel their child is being forced into a self-contained class or a program that is unacceptable to them. Be as supportive as possible. Think about how difficult this must be for the family. Advocate with them if the school system is moving too slowly.
- If you think the family is neglecting or abusing their child, you have a legal and a moral (I think) obligation to report this information to your principal or director or to the city in which you work. You are not helping a child by ignoring the problem.
- Seek out help for a special needs or a difficult child. You may have to wait months, or you may never get support services for a child. While you are waiting, seek out temporary forms of help.

How to Get Help

What can you do if you have too many special needs children and not enough adults to help? Usually, a special needs child can receive services through the Division of Special Education, but only if they have been evaluated and services are recommended. Often, you will have a number of children who have special needs that may not meet the requirements for the types of special services offered by your school district. This leaves you in a difficult position because it is so difficult to help both the children who are most needy and the rest of the class.

You may have to find your own resources; here are some ways to accomplish this.

- Get a parent or other family member from the class to work with you. Perhaps that person can work with or spend time with the child. You can read in *Classroom Interviews* about Dora Cruz, the grandmother of a student in my class. Dora volunteered in our classroom for three years. She was fantastic with special needs children. She was like a mother, a friend, and a teacher to them.
- Ask the administration for extra help—a volunteer, a teacher's aide, a mainstream paraprofessional, a guidance counselor, a social worker.
- Find out from colleagues or the guidance counselor where there may be special services or counseling in the community, particularly free or low-cost services.
- If the child is particularly difficult or disruptive, arrange for the child to go for a period of time each day to another class or to assist a librarian or other person in the school so you can get some relief.
- If the child is particularly difficult during lunch or recess (often a difficult time for children with problems) make arrangements for the child to be with an administrator or in another class so that the child can get through that period of time without stress.

How to Get a Child Evaluated

This is usually a difficult and frustrating process because of the bureaucracy in the system. Every school system has their own legal procedures, so check with the staff in your school to find out what you are required to do. Here are some general suggestions:

- Keep an anecdotal record on a daily basis. There may be problems with speech or hearing, processing information, and other learning problems. Or there may be emotional problems. Record as much information as possible. These are your own private records. You may want to share this information with the family and the staff at your school.
- Speak with colleagues, including the child's previous teacher(s) to learn more about the child. Ask for suggestions.
- Speak informally with an administrator to learn more about the child. Ask for suggestions and help.

- Speak to the family. Remember, you are talking about their child, their loved one. Be sensitive. Be honest. Tell the family that you will be doing everything possible to get extra help for their child. It's not an easy process for the family, even a family that asks for an evaluation. These meetings are very painful for the family. I find the meetings painful, too, because it's such a blow to the family. If you are certain that the intervention will be in the same school and that the child will stay in a regular classroom or a combined regular/special education class, assure the family of that. This might include speech and language, occupational therapy, resource room, or counseling. One of the biggest fears for families is that their child will be in a self-contained special education program.

- When you are sure that the child needs some intervention that you can't provide, meet with the appropriate personnel at your school to discuss the child and to come up with appropriate interventions. This could be a small reading group, work with a volunteer, Reading Recovery, tutoring, and so on. At MNS, we are required to have such a meeting with the principal and the team that does evaluations. If, after a period of time, these interventions are not effective, there is another meeting. Then, there may be a recommendation for an evaluation.

- Speak again with the family about the proposal for an evaluation. You may want to have another staff member with you if you think it will be too difficult for you to do alone. Explain the procedure for the evaluation. Make sure the family knows their rights. Make sure they know that nothing will happen without their signature—that includes the evaluation and placements in any special education program (resource room, speech and language, physical therapy, counseling, inclusion class, self-contained class, and so on). Assure the family that you will be there for them during the process of evaluation, and that you will make sure their rights are respected.

- Monitor the evaluation. There are legal requirements, including timetables, for each step of the evaluation. Speak to the team or your administration to make sure the requirements are being met. If you feel that the team is insensitive to the child or family, do your best to intervene. The child will most likely remain in your class the whole year. Continue doing your best to give the child as much support as possible during the evaluation process.

Try to Find the Good in a Special Needs Child

As with every child, search for what is special.

- Determine whether the child has a special talent in art, music, science, sports, history, computers, or some other area. Ask the family, the child, and previous teachers.
- Look for books or computer programs related to the child's interests.
- See how you can make room for his interests within your curriculum.
- Try to arrange for lessons in music or art in or outside of school if the child shows a talent or interest.
- Try to arrange for the child to be in a sports program if the child shows an interest in sports or appears to need exercise.
- Seek out after-school arrangements that would be of interest to the child.

In Summary

Clearly, it's best for all when a special needs child has optimal support, whether in a mainstream class, a class that combines regular education and special needs children, or a self-contained class. It's difficult for all when the child is in a class where there are not adequate supports. But, I urge teachers to work to the best of their ability to provide the best quality of education possible for every child.

Conclusion

As the children filed into my classroom on January 17, they took their assigned seats at the neat rows of desks. Some prodded the others to fold their hands and sit up straight so their row would be called on first to hang up their coats in the closet. Row after row when they were called on, they hung up their coats and returned promptly to their seats. There they sat silently and waited for their classmates to finish.

Fifteen minutes later they were ready to begin reading together—*Fun with Dick and Jane*. My hair was pinned neatly into a bun. The children wore white shirts and red ties with pants or skirts. One of the noisier students called out during the lesson and had to write neatly, "I will not talk," five times. Another dunked a girl's hair into the "inkwell" and had to endure a "smack on the hand" with the ruler. They worked their way through the day, as I tapped the desk with the pointer to get their attention.

This really did happen in *our* classroom. And yet, Heinemann still wanted me to write a book for teachers about classroom management. How could this be? Was there a mistake?

My first graders had nearly completed six months of research about a block on Second Avenue, right near our school. Each first grade class at The Manhattan New School had selected a different block on Second Avenue for study. The glorious thing was that we could do the research *our own way*. Our study was based on the children's questions. They wanted to know:

Who lives on the block?
Where do the people come from?
What jobs do the workers do?
How did they make sidewalks?

How did they make the buildings?
How do people on the block travel?
What's under the ground?
What signs are on the block?

They wanted to know what the block was like in the old days. They wanted to know:

What games did people used to play?
What music did they listen to?
What foods did they eat?
How did they get their food?
Where did they go to school?

Especially interesting to the children was the question, "What was our school like in the old days?"

Day after day, for more than three months, we did research to find answers to the questions about the block in modern times. Then, for a month, we refocused our research to what the block and our school (formerly called P.S. 190) were like in the old days. One group of children worked with our student teacher, Mollie Bass, to learn about the desks, the inkwells, the slate boards, the clothes, and the rules. They read books and looked at photos and pictures. The whole class interviewed several grandparents. At an interview of my friend Guy Stewart, we learned about how he used to do yo-yo demonstrations at school yards around the country when he worked for Duncan Yo-Yo in the 1950s. (We found out that a stroke prevented him from doing the two-yo-yo tricks at top speed. That led to further research about strokes, including the reading of Tomie dePaola's *Now One Foot, Now the Other*, an interview of a parent who does research about stroke victims in a poor neighborhood in New York City, and an interview of a parent who is a physician.) Imagine watching yo-yo's "walk the dog" or fly "around the world" in school! For homework children interviewed elderly relatives, family friends, or neighbors. Learning was really fun.

After months of research, we took a trip back into history. We turned our room into a classroom in our school in the "old, old days." The whole day was a role-play. The day before this event, we worked together to roll up the carpet at story circle, and we hid the block area, the pattern blocks, and Legos. Boaz Vaadia, a sculptor and parent from a previous class, made slate boards for each child. A parent made red ties based on pictures from books and a picture of my then ninety-three-year-old father when he was only four years old. We dismantled our hexagon-shaped worktables (made from two trapezoids) and made rows of tables, all facing the blackboard. Children cut black circles for pretend inkwells. We placed name cards in alphabetical order on the desks. We had to use a portable slate board we found and made another with black contact paper because our real slate blackboards had been covered with dry mark boards ten years ago. Our former principal and former superintendent of District 2, Shelley Harwayne, even lent us a copy of *Fun with Dick and Jane*, a collector's item.

Lena's mother, Sharon, took time off from work that day and volunteered to be the art teacher. She helped our city children draw the "perfect" suburban house, as she drew a rectangle, they drew a rectangle, she drew a triangle roof, and they drew a triangle roof, leaving not a moment for self-expression.

The high point of our day was lunch at Jackson Hole, located on the block we were studying. The restaurant has an old-fashioned look. Many family members joined us for lunch and were thrilled to pump their quarters into the jukebox. Some of us even danced in the aisles.

The entire day, we reenacted the old days, including the *discipline*. How difficult it was for me to do that. Some of it was based on memories of my childhood teachers in Buffalo, New York. Some was based on our research. All day I was acting—making children sit with hands folded as they waited to use the coat closet or the lunch line, having them wait in long lines to use the bathroom, rapping on the desk with the pointer, making the whole class read *Dick and Jane* in unison, and more. Part of me kept laughing; part of me was troubled. As I acted, I was doing research about this day of role-playing.

What Did I Conclude from My Research?

I felt so powerful that day. Wow, I was really in charge of every move the children made.

I felt uncomfortable with this kind of power arrangement.

The children were powerless.

There was so much time wasted waiting: waiting to use the closet, waiting to get in line, waiting to use the bathroom.

There was so much waiting and therefore so much less time for teaching or learning.

There were some huge things missing:

the spontaneity

the questions

the delightful detours of an inquiry classroom

the interrelatedness of the different subject areas in the curriculum

the empowerment of the children

William Butler Yeats, the Irish poet and dramatist, said that education is not filling a pail, but "lighting a fire." If we view teaching as filling children with information or "filling an empty pail," we can simply arrange the tables in rows as we did in our role-play, hand out the textbooks, provide lectures, have practice drills in workbooks, and then hand out the tests. We can teach rote art as Lena's mother did for us. We can hand out new versions of basal readers. We can "buy into" single methods of teaching reading or math.

To simply "fill the pail," teachers have to put a certain management system in place. In fact, you will often hear teachers say, "I don't do any teaching the first several weeks. We practice the rules over and over. Then I can teach."

If we are simply "filling an empty pail," we don't need to know that "Sarah's" parents are going through a divorce or that Tommy's father is a building superintendent and his mother cleans Rockefeller Center at night and is not home to help him with his schoolwork. The children must learn to behave properly, to pay attention to the teacher so that they can *receive* the information. Order and control must be imposed.

An Inquiry Classroom—Empowering Children

Our approach to learning is through inquiry, using prior knowledge, asking questions, and seeking answers. The children's questions and critical thinking drive the curriculum. So, the children need to be empowered to take over some of the traditional jobs of the teacher—both the teaching and the discipline.

Working closely with the families is so important in this process. In our community of learners it does matter that "Sarah's" parents are going through a divorce because "Sarah" will need lots of support. In our class it will help to know that Aaron is the youngest of seven children, and that there's lots happening in the home. His parents are juggling work, household responsibilities, doctor visits, and so much more. How did it help to know that Tommy's father is a building superintendent and his mother cleans Rockefeller Center at night? His parents, with their busy work schedule, were not part of the school community. They didn't have much time to help him during the week. It would be important to find a way to get them involved.

In our inquiry classroom the children are empowered to:

- ask questions that will truly drive and shape the curriculum
- think critically
- do research

- work cooperatively to construct knowledge from their experiences and activities at home and at school rather than have facts simply imposed by the teacher or textbook
- be in charge of and responsible for their own behavior, with adults guiding them and stepping in only when necessary

Closing Thoughts

This sounds so easy. I know it is not. It has taken quite a while for inquiry to become the center of my teaching and to develop the classroom management skills to make it work. I can't think of anything more difficult than being a new teacher. If only I knew then what I know now after thirty-one years of teaching. I hope what I have shared in my book will ease the journey for both you and your students as you seek to empower your children, to give them voice, to encourage them to "be your own teacher, to be in charge of your learning and your behavior." I sincerely hope that this book will help you with classroom management so that you can move more quickly to experience the joys of teaching.

Bibliography and Resources

Professional Books

Armstrong, T. 2000. Preface by H. Gardner. *Multiple Intelligences in the Classroom*. Alexandria, VA: Association for Supervision and Curriculum Development.

Edwards, C., L. Gandini, and G. Forman. 1998. *The Hundred Languages of Children: The Reggio Emilia Approach—Advanced Reflections*. 2d ed. Greenwich, CT: Ablex.

Evertson, C., E. Emmer, and M. Worsham. 2000. *Classroom Management for Elementary Teachers*. 5th ed. Boston: Allyn and Bacon.

Harwayne, S. 1999. *Going Public, Priorities and Practices at The Manhattan New School*. Portsmouth, NH: Heinemann.

———. 2000. *Lifetime Guarantees, Toward Ambitious Literacy Teaching*. Portsmouth, NH: Heinemann.

Heard, G. 1999. *Awakening the Heart, Exploring Poetry in Elementary and Middle School*. Portsmouth, NH: Heinemann.

Hemphill, C. 2002. *New York City's Best Public Elementary Schools: A Parents' Guide*. New York: Teachers College.

Rogovin, P. 1998a. *Classroom Interviews: A World of Learning*. Portsmouth, NH: Heinemann.

———. 1998b. *Classroom Interviews in Action*. A video. Portsmouth, NH: Heinemann.

———. 2001. *The Research Workshop: Bringing the World into Your Classroom*. Portsmouth, NH: Heinemann.

Paleontology

Bishop, N. 2000. *Digging for Bird Dinosaurs: An Expedition to Madagascar*. New York: Houghton Mifflin.

151

Dingus, L., and M. Norell, contributor. 1996. *Searching for Velociraptor*. New York: HarperCollins Juvenile Books.

Children's Literature

There are many, many books that could be included in this type of bibliography of children's literature. However, most of the books listed are ones that I have personally used in my classroom to help develop values.

Poetry

Cullinan, B., ed. 1996. *A Jar of Tiny Stars: Poems by NCTE Award-Winning Poets*. Honesdale, PA: Boyds Mills Press.

Giovanni, N. 1985. *Spin a Soft Black Song*. New York: Trumpet Club.

Greenfield, E. 1993. *Nathaniel Talking*. New York: Black Butterfly Children's Group.

———. 1986. *Honey, I Love and Other Love Poems*. New York: HarperCollins.

Gunning, M. 1993. *Not a Copper Penny in Me House: Poems from the Caribbean*. Honesdale, PA: Boyds Mills Press.

Heard, G. 2002. *This Place I Know: Poems of Comfort*. Cambridge, MA: Candlewick Press.

———. 1992. *Creatures of the Earth, Sea, and Sky*. Honesdale, PA: Boyds Mills Press.

Hughes, L. 1994. *The Dream Keeper and Other Poems*. Illus. by B. Pinkney. New York: Scholastic.

Meyers, W. D. 1993. *Brown Angels*. New York: HarperCollins.

Nye, N. S., ed. 1992. *This Same Sky: A Collection of Poems from Around the World*. New York: Simon and Schuster.

Segal, E. 1971. *Be My Friend*. New York: The Citadel Press.

Silverstein, S. 1981. *A Light in the Attic*. New York: Harper and Row.

———. 1974. *Where the Sidewalk Ends*. New York: HarperCollins.

Fiction, Nonfiction, and Historical Fiction

The fiction and historical fiction tend to be useful in read-aloud settings. The nonfiction books tend to be more useful during Research Workshop.

Encouraging Positive Behaviors—Dealing with the Problem of Meanness

Carle, E. 1977. *The Grouchy Ladybug*. New York: Scholastic. (also deals with sharing)

San Souci, R. D. 1989. *The Talking Eggs: A Folktale from the American South*. New York: Dial Books.

Steptoe, J. 1987. *Mufaro's Beautiful Daughters: An African Tale*. New York: Lothrop, Lee & Shepard.

Waber, B. 1973. *Ira Sleeps Over*. New York: Houghton Mifflin. (also deals with believing in ourselves)

Yashima, T. 1976. *Crow Boy*. New York: Puffin.

ENCOURAGING POSITIVE BEHAVIOR—DEALING WITH GREED, VANITY, SPOILED BEHAVIOR, AND SHOWING OFF

Brett, J. 1991. *Berlioz the Bear*. New York: Putnam and Sons.

Goble, P. 1990. *Iktomi and the Ducks, a Plains Indian Story*. New York: Orchard Books.

———. (retold by). 1988. *Iktomi and the Boulder*. New York: Orchard Books.

Kimmel, E. (retold by). 1990. *Anansi and the Moss-Covered Rock*. Illus. by J. Stevens. New York: Holiday House.

Myers, W. D. 1996. *How Mr. Monkey Saw the Whole World*. Illus. by S. Saint James. New York: Delacorte Press, Bantam Doubleday Dell Publishing Group.

Perkins, A. (retold by). No date. *King Midas and the Golden Touch*. Illus. by H. and R. Shekerjian. New York: Scholastic.

Vathanaprida, S. 1998. *The Girl Who Wore Too Much: A Folktale from Thailand*. Illus. by Y. L. Davis. English translation by M. R. MacDonald. Little Rock, AR: August House Little-Folk.

ENCOURAGING POSITIVE BEHAVIORS—DEALING WITH DISHONESTY

Demi. 1990. *The Empty Pot*. New York: Henry Holt and Company.

Littledale, F. 1971. *Peter and the North Wind*, retold from the Norse tale *The Lad Who Went to the North Wind*. Illus. by T. Howell. New York: Scholastic.

Rose, A. (retold by). 1976. *Akimba and the Magic Cow: A Folktale from Africa*. Illus. by H. Meryman. New York: Scholastic.

DEALING WITH POSITIVE BEHAVIORS—LEARNING TO FOLLOW THE RULES

Troughton, J. 1986. *Tortoise's Dream*. New York: Bedrick/Blackie.

ENCOURAGING POSITIVE BEHAVIORS—DEALING WITH SHARING

Mollel, T. (retold by). 1996. *Ananse's Feast: An Ashanti Tale*. Illus. by A. Glass. New York: Clarion Books.

ENCOURAGING POSITIVE BEHAVIORS—COMBATING RACISM, SEXISM, STEREOTYPES, AND DISCRIMINATION

Adler, D. 1992. *A Picture Book of Jesse Owens*. Illus. by R. Casilla. New York: Holiday House.

Coles, R. 1995. *The Story of Ruby Bridges*. Illus. by G. Ford. New York: Scholastic.

Green, C. 1991. *Elizabeth Blackwell, First Woman Doctor*. Chicago: Children's Press.

Golenbrock, P. 1990. *Teammates*. Illus. by P. Bacon. New York: Scholastic.

Hoffman, M. 1991. *Amazing Grace*. Illus. by C. Binch. New York: Scholastic.

King Mitchell, M. 1994. *Uncle Jed's Barbershop*. Illus. by J. Ransome. New York: Scholastic.

Lindbergh, R. 1996. *Nobody Owns the Sky: The Story of "Brave Bessie" Coleman*. Illus. by P. Paparone. Cambridge, MA: Candlewick.

Louie, A.-L. 1996. *Yeh-Shen*. New York: Puffin.

Marzollo, J. 1993. *Happy Birthday, Martin Luther King*. Illus. by B. Pinkney. New York: Scholastic.

Surat, M. M. *Angel Child, Dragon Child*. Illus. by B.-D. Mai. New York: Scholastic. (about a Vietnamese child coming to live in the United States)

ENCOURAGING POSITIVE BEHAVIOR—FRIENDSHIP, LOVE, WORKING TOGETHER, AND TAKING CARE OF OTHERS

Bang, M. 1985. *The Paper Crane*. New York: Greenwillow.

Bunting, E. 1997. *A Day's Work*. Illus. by R. Himler. New York: Houghton Mifflin. (the immigrant experience, finding enduring values)

———. 1989. *The Wednesday Surprise*. Illus. by D. Carrick. New York: Clarion.

Cowen-Fletcher, J. 1994. *It Takes a Village*. New York: Scholastic.

dePaola, T. 1981. *Now One Foot, Now the Other*. New York: Putnam Sons.

DiSalvo-Ryan, D. 1997. *Uncle Willie and the Soup Kitchen*. New York: Mulberry.

Fox, M. 1988. *Koala Lou*. New York: Harcourt Brace & Company.

Freeman, D. 1978. *A Pocket for Corduroy*. New York: Puffin Books.

Gerson, M. (retold by). 1994. *How Night Came from the Sea: A Story from Brazil*. Illus. by C. Golembe. New York: Little, Brown and Company.

Gilman, P. 1992. *Something from Nothing*. New York: Scholastic.

Lionni, L. 1973. *Swimmy*. New York: Knopf. (also see other books by Leo Lionni)

McDermott, G. 1988. *Anansi the Spider: A Tale from the Ashanti*. New York: Henry Holt and Company.

Pomerantz, C. 1993. *If I Had a Paka: Poems in Eleven Languages*. Illus. by N. Tafuri. New York: William Morrow.

Rylant, C. 1992. *An Angel for Solomon Singer*. Illus. by P. Catalanotto. New York: Orchard Paperbacks.

Steptoe, J. 1997. *Creativity*. Illus. by E. B. Lewis. New York: Houghton Mifflin.

———. 1989. *The Story of Jumping Mouse*. New York: HarperTrophy.

Waber, B. 2000. *Ira Sleeps Over*. Boston: Houghton Mifflin.

Williams, V. B. 2001. *Amber Was Brave, Essie Was Smart: The Story of Amber and Essie Told in Poems and Pictures*. New York: Greenwillow.

———. 1984. *Music, Music for Everyone*. New York: The Trumpet Club.

———. 1983. *Something Special For Me*. New York: Mulberry.

———. 1982. *A Chair for My Mother*. New York: Mulberry.

Encouraging Positive Behaviors—Peaceful Coexistence, Acceptance, Appreciating Others, Love (despite differences)

Hamanaka, S., ed. 1995. *On the Wings of Peace, Writers and Illustrators Speak Out for Peace, in Memory of Hiroshima and Nagasaki*. New York: Clarion.

McGirr, N. "Out of the Dump." Children's Photography Project of Guatemala City.

Pomerantz, C. 1989. *The Chalk Doll*. New York: HarperCollins.

Scheidl, G. M. 1993. *The Crystal Ball*. Illus. by N. Duroussy. Translated by R. Lanning. New York: North-South Books.

Seeger, P., and P. DuBois Jacobs. 2001. *Abyoyo Returns*. Illus. by M. Hays. New York: Simon and Schuster.

Stock, C. 1995. *Guatemala*. New York: Lothrop, Lee & Shepard Books. (about families living in the landfill in Guatemala City)

———. 1993. *Where Are You Going Manyoni?* New York: Morrow Junior Books.

Encouraging Positive Behavior—Acceptance and Support for People with Disabilities

Anderson, H. C. 1995. *The Ugly Duckling*. Adapted and illus. by J. Pinkney. New York: Morrow Junior Books.

Clifton, L. 1992. *Everett Anderson's Friend*. New York: Henry Holt Co.

———. 1980. *My Friend Jacob*. Illus. by T. DiGrazia. New York: Dutton.

Gregory, N. 1997. *How Smudge Came*. Illus. by R. Lightburn. New York: Walker and Company.

Peterson, J. W. 1977. *I Have a Sister, My Sister Is Deaf*. Illus. by D. Kogan Ray. New York: Harper & Row.

Taking Care of the Environment

Cherry, L. 1992. *A River Ran Wild*. New York: Trumpet Club, Bantum Doubleday Dell Publishing Group.

Child Labor and Workers' Rights

Buirski, N. (photographer), H. Cisneros (illustrator), R. Blades (designer). 1994. *Earth's Angels: Migrant Children in America*. San Francisco: Pomegranate Artbooks.

Freedman, R. 1994. *Kids at Work: Lewis Hine and the Crusade Against Child Labor*. New York: Scholastic.

Littlefield, H. 1996. *Fire at the Triangle Factory*. Minneapolis: Carolrhoda Books.

McCully, E. A. 1996. *The Bobbin Girl*. New York: Penguin.

Resources

(for professional books, newsletters, workshops, children's books, activities, curriculum, and videos)

American Federation of Teachers, www.aft.org

Children's Creative Response to Conflict, www.sharingsuccess.org

Coalition of Education Activists, www.nceaonline.org

Educators for Social Responsibility, www.ersmetro.org (New York City); www.ersnational.org (national)

Highsmith. Source of multicultural literature, www.highsmith.com

National Education Association, www.nea.org

Rethinking Schools, www.rethinkingschools.org

Teaching for Change, www.teachingforchange.org

Index